Up-Wingers

Books by F.M. Esfandiary

Up-Wingers

Optimism One

Identity Card

The Beggar

Day of Sacrifice

F. M. Esfandiary

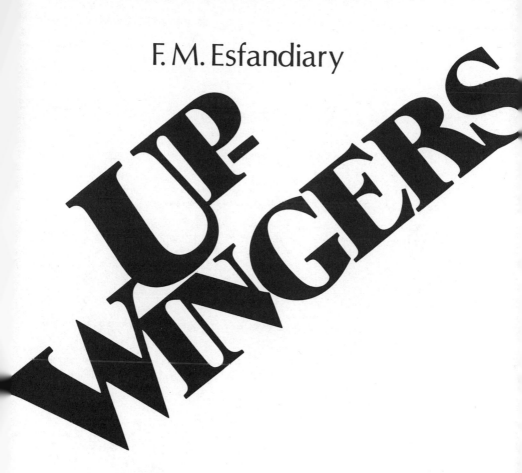

UP-WINGERS

The John Day Company

NEW YORK

Library of Congress Cataloging in Publication Data

Esfandiary, Fereidoun M
    Up-wingers.

    1. Civilization, Modern—1950–   2. Forecasting.
I. Title.
CB428.E73 1973   901.94'7   72-12070
ISBN 0-381-98243-2
ISBN 0-381-90008-8 (pbk.)

The John Day Company, 257 Park Avenue South, New York N.Y. 10010.

Published on the same day in Canada by Longman Canada Limited.

Printed in the United States of America

contents

CONTENTS

introduction

I have often been told that I am *too* optimistic about
the future.

How can anyone be too optimistic?

My regret is that I am not optimistic enough. It is
not possible to project the fantastic worlds which will
continue to open up to us in the coming years.
Worlds which far transcend my most daring optimism.

No one today can be *too* optimistic.

We are daily surging ahead in many areas—biology
genetics physics biochemistry astronomy medicine

surgery fetology communication transportation
food-production computation weather-forecasting
environmental-monitoring international relations
interpersonal relations self-image . . . Advances in
these and many other areas since 1955 have been
more monumental than all the progress in the previous
two thousand years.

Even fifteen years ago many of today's
breakthroughs would have been dismissed as fantasies
—too utopian and optimistic. To us they are already
routine.

This rate of advance is now accelerating. Progress is
faster and more global than ever.

Precisely because of the accelerating rate of change
we urgently need plans for the coming years.

Unfortunately most projections of the future are
pessimistic. Western intellectuals in particular hobbled
by puritan guilt and self-doubts flood the world with
books and films and scenarios foredooming the future.
To them our successes and potentials are not real.
Only our failures.

Their reactionary outlook has helped make people
afraid of progress and the future. "If the future is so
bleak" is the unconscious reasoning "why think about
it? Safer to hide in the womb of the past or of mother
nature."

We must develop a bold new philosophy of the
future. A hopeful outlook which can embolden people
to want to face the future. To want to plan for it.

More than ever we need short-range and long-range
plans. Guidelines to help us steer our onrushing
breakthroughs making them work for all humanity.

In our fluid times however plans and guidelines
(such as I have outlined in this book) cannot be
definitive. Lengthy guidelines may have been possible
in slower times. Today we cannot and should not
even attempt to structure the future through elaborate
plans. Our increasingly fluid times demand fluid
guidelines.

The plans I have worked out here are for the Near
Future and the Middle Future—the next ten twenty
thirty years.

Beyond fifty years from now (beyond the year
2020) is the Far Future. The human situation will have
changed so unrecognizably that it is superfluous to
plan for it now.

In this tract I have bypassed the plodding pace of
print. Most books are too slow for our times.
Up-Wingers, addressed primarily to the fluid, attempts
to approximate the rhythm of electronics. Brief crisp
rapid bursts of ideas intended to inform goad provoke
catalyze . . .

We not only need new ideas and visions—but also
need new ways to communicate them.

F.M. Esfandiary

part 1

cosmic upheaval on planet earth

A cosmic upheaval is now surging on Planet Earth.
We are at a major evolutionary milestone.
2 billion years ago the emergence of life in the oceans.
400 million years ago the emergence of life on land.
70 million years ago the primates.
3 million years ago the rise of ape-men.
35,000 years ago the emergence of humanoids.
Today the emergence of a new concept of life which is—

>   1. evolving beyond the animal-human.
>   2. extending beyond Planet Earth.

This Cosmic Upheaval is one of the most extraordinary developments in the entire evolution of life on this planet. The last evolutionary leap of such magnitude occurred millions of years ago.

It is important to understand that some of the breakthroughs now burgeoning all around us are no longer simply historic—but evolutionary.

The asexual creation of new mutants and the emergence of cyborgs are not historic developments. They are evolutionary breakthroughs. The biological upheaval now in its infancy is moving toward radically new concepts of life—beyond animal-human.

The bursts to the moon and to the planets are also not historic events. They are major evolutionary breakthroughs. The Space Age still in its infancy is catapulting us beyond the premises that govern life on this planet. We are witnessing today the very beginning of a cosmic dimension which is not only altering life on this planet but affecting our entire solar system and the universe beyond.

Today when we speak of immortality and of going to another world we no longer mean these in a theological or metaphysical sense. People are now striving for physical immortality. People are now traveling to other worlds.

Transcendence is no longer a metaphysical concept. It has become reality.

These new dimensions in human life defy all our philosophies, all our social economic political systems, all our age-old concepts of life and nature, Time and Space.

Until now human civilizations throughout the ages have been predicated on the same fixed premises—

Nature governs all life on this planet.
We are bound by the laws of evolution.
We are confined to flesh and blood bodies.
We are permanently confined to this planet.
We are finite—we are born and we die.

Today so far as we know for the first time since the emergence of life on this planet all these premises are being challenged.

We have no philosophy no ideology no conceptual or social system to accommodate this emerging dimension.

This new cosmic dimension defies *all* our human traditions.

We now need new conceptual frameworks and new visions to guide us as we venture into uncharted spheres which are potentially full of hope.

up-wingers

To transcend more rapidly to higher levels of evolution we must begin by breaking out of the confinement of traditional ideologies.

We are at all times slowed down by the narrowness of Right-wing and Left-wing alternatives. If you are not conservative you are liberal if not right of center you are left of it or middle of the road.

Our traditions comprise no other alternatives. There is no ideological or conceptual dimension *beyond* conservative and liberal *beyond* Right and Left.

Right and Left—even the extreme Left—are traditional frameworks predicated on traditional premises striving in obsolete ways to attain obsolete goals.

The premises of the entire Left are indistinguishable from those of the entire Right. The extreme Left is simply a linear extension of the extreme Right. The liberal is simply a more advanced conservative, the radical Left a more advanced liberal. You can move farther and farther Left to the most radical Left, you will still be advancing within an intrinsically orthodox framework.

It is no longer only the Right that is conservative. The entire Left is also suddenly conservative. The liberal and the radical Left have fallen behind. But they will not face their new conservatism. They resist and attack the new breakthroughs—the more they resist the more conservative they grow and therefore the more cynical.

There is no cynicism more bitter than that of liberals or radical Left-wingers who sense that they have fallen behind the times.

They still like to view themselves and are viewed by others as progressive. This is precisely where the danger lies. This is one of the main reasons for resistances to more rapid progress. In the name of progress the liberal and the radical Left-winger resist progress. They resist because the new breakthroughs do not fit into their highly structured frameworks and confined goals.

The Space Program? That is a waste of money, they protest. The money ought to be spent on more important things.

Genetic Engineering? That is dehumanizing. It will lead to push-button people.

New concepts of reproduction such as out-of-the-womb? That is hideously impersonal mechanical.

Modern technology? Dehumanizing. It is robbing us of privacy and individuality, upsetting the balance of nature.

Every breakthrough is viewed as a threat. Every new idea viciously attacked as *anti-human simplistic utopian.*

The Right-Left establishment is fighting a losing battle. It is following in the footsteps of earlier traditionalists who resisted the more modest breakthroughs of the past.

Those earlier traditionalists were also sure that giving women the right to vote would upset the laws of nature. That the camera and the telephone would do away with privacy. That birth control and planned parenthood were impersonal dehumanizing. That television was an "idiot box" etc. . . . etc. . . .

It is particularly important to recognize that the liberal and the radical Left are the new gradualists— the new conservatives. I stress the point because this liberalism and Left radicalism masquerading in the name of progress are putting up the strongest resistances to the newest breakthroughs.

What effrontery calling themselves progressive. What self-delusion. Those who do not believe in progress or in the future have not deserved the right to call themselves progressive.

There are whole new dimensions emerging which go far beyond Right and Left, far beyond conservative and liberal.

These dimensions defy *all* the old labels.

How do you identify Space scientists who this very day are working with new sets of premises to establish communities in other worlds? Are they Right-wing or Left? Are they conservative or liberal?

How do you categorize radio astronomers who are now scanning the galaxies in search of Intelligent Life? Or scientists working on the implantation of devices in the human body enabling the individual to control its own pain and pleasures, emotions and dreams? Or those working on phytotrons and nuclear food plants which can provide endless quantities of food? Or computerers developing cybernated systems which will free people of the primitive ordeals of full-time employment and of bureaucratic government. Or bio-engineers striving to conquer death?

These and other breakthroughs are outside the range of all the traditional philosophical social economic political frameworks. These new dimensions are nowhere on the Right or on the Left. These new dimensions are **Up.**

Up is an entirely new framework whose very premises and goals transcend the conventional Right and Left.

As I will show in this book we are at the beginning of two major upheavals—

1. The Planetary Movement. Through this movement the Up-Winger wants to do away with age-old social systems. What are these systems? Biological parenthood marriage family school money work bureaucratic-government nations. Not simply to modernize these archaic systems—to do away with them altogether.

The Right-Left revolutionary for instance wants to

overthrow a government. The Up-Winger wants to overthrow the very concept of bureaucratic government replacing it with cybernated systems.

2. The Cosmic Upheaval. Here the Up-Winger proceeds from the premise that we are now ascending to a higher evolution and that therefore it is no longer enough to resolve age-old social economic political problems—we must urgently overcome the more basic tyrannies of nature the arbitrariness of evolution the limitations of the human body the confinements of Time and Space.

It is the human situation that is basically tragic. Right-Left revolutions cannot alter this basic dilemma. For instance the most revolutionary Left-wing group has no program to overcome death. The entire Right-Left establishment is still death-oriented.

Space programs and biological advances in capitalist and socialist countries are outgrowths of modern science and technology—not of Right-wing or Left-wing ideologies. We are extending ourselves in Space and in Time not *because* of capitalism or socialism but *in spite* of them.

The Right-Left Capitalist-Socialist establishments have used their Space programs chiefly to advance their nationalistic militaristic hangups. They still do not comprehend the *evolutionary* impact of the Space dimension.

The Right-Left establishment is psychologically and ideologically unprepared for our emerging situation in Time and Space. It is not surprising that much of the Right-Left is vehemently opposed to this new cosmic dimension.

The Right-Left establishment wants to maintain an evolutionary status quo. It is resigned to humanity's basic predicament. It simply strives to make life better within this predicament.

Up-Wingers are resigned to nothing. They accept no human predicament as permanent no tragedy as irreversible no goals as unattainable.

To be Up you must sever all ideological ties with the Right-Left establishment. You must make a break with the traditional concept of linear historical progress. That is now too slow and limited.

You must be prepared to quantum-leap forward. This means starting with a new set of premises new visionary aims.

In the coming years you will hear much about the Up-dimension. Right and Left will become irrelevant. Conservatism liberalism Left-wing radicalism will continue to become indistinguishable—they are *all* conservative. They are all Down.

This tract is a guideline for the up-coming Up.

optimism

the cosmic dimension

We not only need a new ideological thrust. We also need a new philosophical outlook.

Guidelines for action are useless if there is no commitment. There can be no commitment if there is no will no self-esteem no hope.

In my book *Optimism One* I explained some of the reasons for our age-old pessimism. The ones I developed are—

1. Lack of self-esteem. Until a few years ago children the world over grew up in destitution or in

repressive overprotective environments. The orientation to failure began early in life. Nothing ever works out for me became generalized into the lifelong pessimistic philosophy that nothing ever works out for anyone that there is no progress that nothing ever really changes or can be made to change.

2. The second factor is guilt arising from puritan upbringing. Until recent times people—particularly in Western cultures—were brought up with the conviction that they were wicked and did not *deserve* happiness or success. As adults such people are unlikely to rejoice in human success and progress. Even if personally successful they maintain a philosophy of pessimism and failure. Optimism hope happiness progress evoke in them a sense of guilt impelling them to dwell on failures.

3. Lack of historical perspective. Until recently people did not have opportunities to see first hand different cultures at varying levels of historical development. Feudal societies were not aware that other peoples had advanced and that therefore it was possible to advance. While industrial peoples were seldom aware of the primitivism and backwardness in other lands. People the world over could not experience the movement of history and therefore felt that nothing was changing.

4. Finally our legacy of theological and philosophical pessimism. Throughout the ages people were conditioned by theologies and philosophies of

Submission Resignation Fatalism Nihilism Despair
Nothingness etc. . . . . These theologies and
philosophies were logical since our human situation
was tragic—limited by Time and Space. Even recent
visionaries like Marx Nietzsche Freud and the
evolutionists were justifiably resigned to the
inevitability of human mortality and the limiting
confinement to this planet. It is therefore
understandable that during our entire history there has
never been a philosophy of Optimism based on an
open-ended future.

I am aware that other factors have helped sustain
pessimism. For instance genetic disposition to life-long
depression.
Whatever the reasons pessimism as a philosophy
was at one time logical. Today it is not.
We have reached a stage in our evolution at which
pessimism fatalism are no longer rational philosophies.
Today Optimism is the only relevant outlook.
This is the very first time in evolution at which a
philosophy of optimism is possible.
Ours is the First Age of Optimism. We are at
Optimism One.

What is the meaning of the philosophy of
Optimism? How can we make this philosophy work
for us?
**Optimism as a philosophy is squarely predicated
on one central development: our emerging
situation in Time and Space.**
Suddenly the barriers are coming down.
Suddenly humankind's situation is not

circumscribed or limited. Not intramundane and not finite.

For the very first time our potentials have become totally limitless. Our future open-ended.

Everything is now suddenly possible. Everything attainable.

As I will explain in Part 3 we are breaking out of elemental confinements to extend ourselves throughout All-Time and All-Space. We are on our way to becoming Universal and Eternal.

Without these new cosmic dimensions Optimism is meaningless. Social economic political progress does not by itself justify a philosophy of optimism.

So long as we were hopelessly doomed to a brief period in Time and trapped within a small speck in Space, all our social economic political freedoms and amenities were limited and ultimately meaningless.

This is precisely the distinction between the new optimism and the optimism of the visionaries of the past. The optimism of a Goethe a Nietzsche or a Marx was necessarily a limited optimism based on historical progress. It was an optimism within a basically pessimistic human situation.

But the optimism I have been advancing is not based simply on historical progress. It is primarily and ultimately predicated on our evolutionary breakthroughs.

To miss this central point is to miss the whole meaning of Optimism.

In our preoccupation with daily domestic problems we tend all too often to lose sight of these transcendent dimensions now opening up to us. It is therefore not surprising that we persist in our traditional posture of pessimism.

But the philosophy of an age cannot and must not be derived from daily newspaper headlines. Headlines which invariably stress our daily problems.

An age cannot be defined by the detail of everyday events. The broader currents are what finally mark an age.

These broad and ever broadening currents mark ours as the First Age of Optimism.

We must now make this philosophy of Optimism work for us. We need Optimism as infusion to accelerate our forward thrust, uplift our self-image.

Until now we have been passive organisms manipulated by the arbitrary forces of evolution tyrannized by the rapacities of nature beaten down by authoritarian social systems (parents teachers employers priests leaders gods) enfeebled by theologies and philosophies which have instilled in us the conviction that we are evil and worthless.

These age-old pressures have left us limp.

Not surprisingly therefore our gravest crisis now as in the past is the lack of self-esteem. We lack self-esteem as individuals and as a species.

Today we are challenging our old passivity, emerging as creators of our own destiny. One of the greatest upheavals now unfolding is in our human role in evolution.

But our new activism in the universe is not bolstering our self-image rapidly enough. We are still hobbled by our traditional self-image—viewing ourselves as puny and passive.

We need a massive infusion of confidence—a cosmic consciousness-uplifting.

Optimism as a philosophy strives to provide this bolstering. It seeks to update our self-image rendering it compatible with our exploding role in the universe.

One way to achieve consciousness-raising is to travel all over our planet—the earlier in life the better. To experience first hand the peoples and the animals the ruins and the launching pads the mountains the oceans and the deserts—to become involved in our planet. Its past present and future. In this way develop the awareness that we are not simply members of some community religion or nation. Or simply a part of a specific place and a specific time. But that we are members of this entire human family, creatures of this entire planet, part of a dynamic continuity—an ongoing forward-thrusting evolution whose origins go back to the animals the forests the oceans but whose potentials are now suddenly infinite.

A second step in this uplifting is to grow involved in the universe. We can do this effectively at night in the country when the universe is most visible.

People who live in cities are too preoccupied with everyday problems too blinded by city lights to look out at the universe and develop a cosmic awareness. Rural people living under the nightly roof of galaxies lack the scope to look beyond their sheds and villages.

At night in the country we can experience the moon the planets the stars and the galaxies. At first the exposure may be disquieting. But gradually as we grow more and more involved the universe grows familiar and reassuring.

It is then that we can slowly realize who we really

are. Not simply members of a neighborhood or a nationality. But members of a remarkably intelligent species inhabiting a planet in this solar system this galaxy this universe. A part of a Space-Time dimension greater and more transcendent than anything on the streets.

It may then occur to us that our brain—this human brain of ours poised there observing the galaxies—is one of the extraordinary phenomena in the universe.

We can further cosmicalize our consciousness by involving ourselves in the monumental breakthroughs now burgeoning all around us. Breakthroughs in inter-people and inter-nation communications. Particularly upheavals in biology and space which as I will show in Part 3 are transforming our situation in the universe.

All these and other attempts at consciousness-uplifting are intended to liberate us from our traditional self-image. Help us grow aware that we are part of something greater than our everyday existences. That from here on we can and we will achieve the most transcendent visions. That there is hope—a new hope in the world.

This new Up-Wing spirit must now infuse all our movements. No movement can succeed if it does not believe in its success. No leadership is worth anything if it does not dare project hope.

You cannot energize people by generating self-doubt —maybe we will succeed maybe we won't. This is half-assed leadership.

It takes guts to be optimistic.

It also takes monumental energy because the majority of humankind traumatized by guilt fear self-doubt lives off the life force of the visionary-optimists.

Anger over our lingering problems is fine. Anger can be a positive force. But pessimism defeatism—never.

Pessimism is reactionary and leads to apathy. "What is the use" the pessimist reasons "human nature is hopelessly evil the world is rotten—why try? The hell with the world. I will think only of myself."

It is no accident that those who complain the most about the world are the ones who do the least.

If you are doing nothing for the world you have no moral right to complain. You have not even earned the right to be pessimistic.

Don't listen to the pessimists and the cynics. They are losers.

They don't even feel they *deserve* happiness.

If we had listened to them we would still be in caves.

Don't listen to those who say it can't be done. Remember the pessimists throughout the centuries who were absolutely sure that the world was about to end. Remember those who were absolutely sure that conquests and colonialism would never end. That we would never have a United Nations that Common Markets would never succeed that global communication would never happen . . . That we would never have a six-day workweek that we would never have a five-day workweek never a four-day workweek . . . That life expectancy could never go beyond forty never beyond fifty never beyond sixty never beyond seventy . . . That we could never be like birds and fly that we could never reach the moon that we could never that we would never that we will never . . .

I am fed up with these messengers of doom.

Don't listen to those who say it can't be done. Listen to those who say it can be done.

Listen to the optimists. Optimism appeals to the noblest emotions—idealism trust confidence. Pessimism appeals to the basest—guilt shame fear self-doubt self-hate.

Optimism is visionary. Pessimism reactionary. Pessimism is Anti-Future.

The whole history of humanity is irrefutable proof of the triumph of optimism over pessimism. The triumph of the doers over the withholders. The triumph of individuals with burning visions who through the ages have been prodding and pushing their fellow humans up and up from the abyss from one level of history to the next.

Today we are preparing to take giant evolutionary leaps into fantastic beautiful worlds. There is no room for pessimism no room for the Old World psychology of despair. We have come too far triumphed over too many impossible barriers disproven too many timid alarmists to allow ourselves now to remain bogged down in negativism.

For the very first time we have the ability and the resources to resolve *all* our age-old problems. More important we have the potential to up-wing to a higher evolution.

What we need today is intelligent planning commitment vision. With these we can now achieve anything.

part 2

the planetary movement

The planetary movement is an extension of humanity's age-old struggle with the terrestrial environment. It is a departure from previous revolutions because:

1. It is global—issuing from large urban centers and spreading across the planet.

2. Its aim is not simply to modernize the old social economic political institutions. But to do away with them altogether.

What will take the place of procreation family marriage school art work money agriculture government city nation? In this section I will discuss these questions and project some new directions.

beyond family

the universal process

We are all under the impact of millennia of conditioning. We feel impelled to have a family. Impelled to have children. Impelled to have a home. Impelled to send children to school. Impelled . . . impelled . . .

We accept these traditions as incontrovertible. Consider them biological imperatives seldom questioning them more deeply. Do you really need a family at all? Do you really need marriage? Do you need children? A home? A school?

The craving for marriage family home is chiefly a

craving for structure. This craving probably begins in the mother's womb—the first structure.

(There is not much we can do *now* about this earliest structure. Within forty or fifty years we will probably do away with procreation altogether. We will perpetuate life in the living and this pathological craving for womb-structures may be slowly deprogrammed out of us. Still later future-people may not crave any structures—not even planets.)

If the womb is the first structure the second is the family. But in providing a kind of womb-like security the family in reality perpetuates in the individual lifelong vulnerability to *insecurity*. The structure-dependence which the infant had developed in the womb is reinforced by the family.

We may not now be able to do anything about the womb but there is much we can do right away about the family.

Today in urban centers around the planet age-old institutions of family marriage home are breaking down. In the cities where trends often start the direction is away from marriage and family. Urbanites now marry later than ever enjoy more freedom within marriage and divorce with greater ease and frequency.

Attempts are under way to modernize marriage— Trial-marriage serial-marriage group-marriage open-marriage celibate-marriage . . .

These timid gropings do not go to the roots of our family problems.

Those who advocate these alternatives are like the reformers within the church. Reforms are no longer enough. Marriage itself must go.

Marriage in any form is an inherently primitive system. No variation will work. You cannot modernize such a system. It is like striving to modernize religion or the army.

All family systems are monopolistic and exclusivist. This is true of the extended-family the polygamous and polyandrous families the nuclear family the Kibbutz the cooperative the commune. The exclusivity varies in degrees.

In recent decades the nuclear family (father mother children) has been supplanting the older family systems. Throughout much of the twentieth century the insistent thesis of Western social scientists has been this: If a child feels loved by its mother and father it will have a solid emotional foundation. It will grow up secure. A good relationship with the all-important mother and father is essential to the child's healthy development.

This emphasis on positive parent-child relations pervades our consciousness our whole cultural matrix. Particularly in modern and Western societies.

The fact is that the *premise* of this quasi-modern thesis is wrong. **The very exclusivity of parent-child relationships is unsound. Even where the parent is loving the relationship is intrinsically unsound. The damage is built into the exclusivity of the relationship between parent and child.**

The infant is early conditioned to the realization that its survival depends on its relationship with the all-important mother. (Or specific mother substitutes.) It is at this earliest stage that the child is conditioned to predicate its survival on a one-to-one relationship. Without *my mother* I will die.

My mother. This is the first act of possessiveness. It

means survival to the infant. But long after its survival-linked value has been outgrown its *imprint* persists and is transferred to others.

Without my mother I will die develops into; without my wife (or my husband or lover) I will die. (The husband or male lover is usually a *mother* symbol— Mother the primary and ultimate figure.) Breakups between lovers are painful precisely because the relationship is often a symbolic replay of that very first mother-child relationship. Losing the husband wife or lover regenerates the infantile terror and trauma at suddenly losing the all-important mother.

I haven't heard from him since his postcard ten days ago. I don't know what to do. I can't concentrate on anything. I can't sleep. I can't eat . . .

She walked out of my life. I don't know what to do without her. Life isn't worth living anymore. I don't want to go anywhere, see anyone . . .

He doesn't want me anymore. He is in love with another woman. I've never been more miserable in my life. I have nightmares. I cry all the time. I wish I were dead . . .

Loneliness bitterness depression hysteria trauma beatings killings suicide. All because of love—fixated love. Fixated on that initial survival-linked love of the mother which leaves the individual forever vulnerable.

All this suffering makes no sense. In a world full of people it makes no sense that we suffer loneliness depression or panic over the disruption of one relationship.

The exclusivity of the mother-child relationship automatically makes every mother possessive. Even the unpossessive mother is possessive.

One of my students summed up the universal feelings of mothers and fathers. "I am not at all a possessive mother" she said. "I give my child a lot of freedom. But there is something beautiful about having my own child. Someone who belongs to me. Not until you have had your own child can you appreciate this."

My own child. Someone who belongs to me. Your own child.

This is the beginning of possessiveness. The parent owns its child. Society expects and accommodates this ownership.

But in possessing a child you create in it the lifelong need to possess and the lifelong need to be possessed.

To possess a child is to render it dependent on your continued possession. In other words to make it possessive.

Being possessed by the parent becomes equated with being loved (assured of survival). To maintain this love the child and later the adult will stop at nothing. It will compete fight grab cheat. Or as I already noted it will withdraw into depression and trauma. As an adult he/she may even kill for this love.

The individual who wants to possess and be possessed is never free never at peace.

Conflicts among people have not been spurred so much by hatred as by love—possessive love exclusive love.

Every day people *kill* for love. They kill or hurt their husbands wives lovers. They kill for the love of the motherland or fatherland. They kill for the love of their clan religion gods.

More people have been killed for *love* than for any other cause.

Patriotism chauvinism ethnocentricism racism—these

are all variations of possessive love. My country my people . . . The initial conditioning to such political and nationalistic exclusivities starts in the exclusive family.

The family based on the initial ownership (possession) of the child is a spawning ground for rivalry jealousy acquisitiveness fanaticism violence . . .

The love we develop in our exclusive family systems is too desperate and fragile. It is a narrow vulnerable love built on exclusivity not inclusivity.

The family is a disruptive destructive system.

The exclusivity of parent-child relations is damaging in more obvious ways—

The child suffers lifelong psychological damage if the mother or father on whom it depends for trust and security is unstable possessive repressive rejecting . . .

The child often suffers lifelong trauma (depression apathy loss of confidence . . .) if the parent suddenly dies or departs.

The child suffers if the parents split up.

It suffers if it is not given freedom.

It also suffers if it is given freedom because within its intrinsically unfree exclusive relationships with its parents freedom is often viewed as rejection.

The child suffers from the inevitable rivalries with its exclusive brothers and sisters who are also involved in exclusive relationships with the all-important parents.

Within family systems parents are too central and all-important to the development of the child rendering the child highly vulnerable, its lifelong well-being on shaky pre-conditions. We have placed all our eggs in one basket.

We must settle for nothing less than the total elimination of the family. The family in its many forms is primitive based on the ownership of individuals— starting with the ownership of children.

We are striving to eliminate economic monopolism. We must also do away with psychological monopolism.

If you are a parent you are a monopolizer of human life.

You are a monopolist whether you are a gentle loving parent or a cruel one.

You are a monopolist because you *own* your child.

Ownership of children is more insidious than the monopoly of wealth and of power.

To have a child of your own and clamor for socialism is inconsistent and self-defeating because you yourself are engaged in the most primitive form of capitalism—psychological monopolism.

To be involved in Women's Liberation and still want a child of your own is inconsistent and self-defeating because you yourself are helping perpetuate the very conditions leading to patriarchy and matriarchy.

To have a child of your own and complain of male chauvinism or any chauvinism is hypocritical because you yourself are guilty of the most insidious form of chauvinism—parenthood.

To liberate women and men we must begin by liberating children.

We must mount a Children's Liberation Movement.

To liberate children means doing away with exclusive parenthood. It means doing away with

the whole corrupt and primitive tradition of having your own child.

What must take the place of biological parenthood family marriage? How will we reproduce? Who will take care of children?

As the old family systems are breaking down two trends are emerging. Single living and communal living.

Living alone is a new concept. It is a rejection of age-old patterns of tribal and family life. A rejection of monopolizations and exclusivities inherent to all kinship ties.

Singling is an attempt to assert independence and achieve fluidity. A way of maximizing opportunities to maintain psychological sexual professional economic political freedoms. The individual is surfacing as never before.

Precisely because of its newness some singlers are having difficulties breaking away from the age-old conditioning to family life. Loneliness boredom estrangement are problems some experience as they learn to make the transition to the new universal life.

A more serious problem is posed by the singler—usually a woman—who wants a child. In urban centers it is increasingly easy for an unmarried unattached woman to have a child. Or what is more common to have a child or two then divorce the husband.

The single mother has renounced the hangups of family and marriage but she deludes herself that she brings up her child free. "I am very good with my child" many a single mother says. "I am not possessive. I want my child to grow up free."

This rationalization is based on a dangerous fallacy. The child brought up by a single mother is anything but free. It is in fact a deeply monopolized child. Here again as I have already pointed out the possessiveness or exclusivity is grooved into the mother-child relationship. It is precisely in such a totally one-to-one relationship that the child is conditioned to fixate on the mother and go through life transfixed.

The single mother no matter how gentle and loving perpetuates the most injurious aspects of the exclusivist family systems.

The single mother is a flagrant monopolizer of human life.

She strives to mollify her own insecurities by seeking security in her exclusive relationship with her own her very own possession—her child.

This is supreme selfishness.

It makes no sense to renounce the monopolism of family and marriage only to turn around and monopolize a child. A child is not an object.

This latest form of psychological monopolism must stop. As I will show there are now alternatives for the singler who wants children.

Communal life is also spreading particularly among modern youngsters. This pattern will continue to spread from urban centers to small towns from advanced societies to the more backward family-oriented societies.

There are many kinds of communes. Some comprised of monogamous units while others more advanced encourage greater communalism in relationships.

The modern commune is a vast improvement over

the old exclusivist family systems. It is the first break with hereditarianism. In the modern commune the members *choose* their fellow communards. They are not foisted on one another by coincidences of biological birth. Partly because choices are made voluntarily rather than imposed and the fact that commune members did not as a rule grow up together the monopolizing forces of guilt and pathological loyalties are minimized.

Contrary to popular belief the modern commune is not a return to the old communes and extended families. Those were highly structured systems in which relationships were never voluntary but imposed. In which guilt shame fear loyalty made for absolute exclusivity from which there was no escape. The child was conditioned to feel that it *belonged* to the extended family. The child was also very aware of its own biological mother and father. Its relationship with them was an exclusivity within an exclusivity. The child was pegged not only to its mother and father but also to the entire clan or family.

Extended families and collectives of the past are not the answer. But the modern commune is a step in the right direction.

At this stage however modern communes are still too structured. As a rule communards settle too long in one place and within a fixed group. Invariably this leads to some of the exclusivities of the old family systems. This is particularly injurious to commune children.

We must guard against creeping exclusivities within the new communes. Such exclusivities can harden into new forms of structures.

The de-structuring of our societies may at first seem

threatening because we are all molded by structures and therefore feel that we cannot do without them that there will be loneliness chaos disorder.

The fact is that there can be more love more security more freedom and communication in a fluid unstructured world than was ever possible in the old fragmented world of families tribes nations and other structures.

We can already see the trend. In the Old World the individual *belonged* to many structures—a tribe or family an ancestral village an ancestral profession a religion a nation. Today modern individuals have outgrown most of these structures. They would feel very circumscribed by them. They want to grow free and spontaneous exploring and embracing more and more of the world.

The point is that the de-structuring of society must not be viewed as a threat.

Don't be afraid to let go.

Modern communes are part of the trend toward the loosening of structures. But we do not want simply to loosen up structures—we want to do away with them.

Let us begin by de-structuring the commune. Let us strive for a more fluid commune—a trans-commune.

The trans-commune is the nucleus of the emerging trans-planetary life.

To settle in a fixed place with a fixed group of people or in a fixed job is to fester. It is to thwart your potential for growth.

Up-individuals do not *settle* in a home a commune or a homeland. Rather they move and evolve and

transit and shuttle and glide and jet and rocket and
float all over the planet.

They are not part of a commune a home or a
homeland. But part of the whole planet. They are part
of the Universal Process.

**The stage beyond the family beyond the
commune is the Universal Process.**

To be part of the Process is to be involved in a
dynamic unrooted all-inclusive evolution.

This is tomorrow-life which we must initiate today.

Such a highly fluid world cannot accommodate the
slow structured communes of today. In fact we must
begin now by dispensing with the word commune.
The word is too evocative of Old World communes
too often confused with old systems. Above all the
word commune suggests rootedness and stability.
Stability is a rationalization for stagnation.

We need a word suggesting motion and fluidity.

Mobilia.

The mobilia is simply a stopover—any place the
individual who wishes to be unalone may stop at to
be with peers and with children.

In the Middle Future the mobilia will replace homes
families communes. Anyone arriving in any community
anywhere on the planet will be able to stop at any
mobilia without introductions. Stay a few days or
weeks then move on.

The Universal Process can already be seen in action
at modern resort clubs and hotels. In a way these
modern hotels are forerunners of mobilias. People
converge at all times from all parts of the planet stay a
few hours days or weeks enjoy modern conveniences
then lift off for all parts of the world again.

The home or commune was a place you lived in. The mobilia is any place you trans-live through.

The family by its very structure is conservative. The mobilia by its nonstructure dynamic.

The family and the commune foster stability. The mobilia encourages movement.

The family by its exclusivity leads to sluggishness boredom loneliness. The mobilia by its fluidity maximizes growth and aliveness.

The family encourages possessiveness. The mobilia sharing.

The family has been the nucleus of a tradition-bound settled fragmented world. The mobilia is the nucleus of a fluid Universal Process.

To trans-live through mobilias is to be involved in the human family.

How can we accelerate the breakup of the family and the destructuring of the commune to release more and more people into the Universal Process? The Up-Winger who lives singly is already in the planetary mainstream. But for the Up-Winger who wishes to trans-live with others and to have children a brief loose guideline may help.

—You can start a mobilia simply by linking up with a few people and opening up your house or land to the world.

—No one should stay at a mobilia longer than a few days a few weeks or at most a few months. *Six months ought to be the maximum.* Move on. Don't fester. (As people grow more and more trans-planetary this time limit will become superfluous. Up-Wingers themselves will not want to stay long in any one place or with any one group.)

—You can move to another mobilia in the same community or to a mobilia across the planet. You can always go back to a mobilia. Of course it will never be the same because all along new people will be trans-living through.

—In these early stages of the Universal Process you must strive to make the mobilia multi-national and multi-racial. Help start mobilias all over the planet invite peoples of different nations and races to them.

—In these early stages it may also help if you display a sign at the door designating the place as a mobilia. The sign may simply say *Mobilia* or *Universal Process* or it may simply be a symbol such as the peace symbol or the United Nations insignia. This is to help people particularly from faraway places to find mobilias. Each mobilia should also have addresses of other mobilias. Hopefully at a later stage all this won't be necessary. Every house and estate will be a mobilia open to the world.

—The number of people at a mobilia will vary. A mobilia may accommodate three people or three hundred depending on the size of the place and the conveniences. If the mobilia is temporarily full new arrivals can be directed to other mobilias.

—The mobilia should be open to the world not only through the flow of people coming and going but also through other channels of universal communication such as television radio telephone videophone computer two-way TV pocket-laser films microfilms cassettes videotapes etc. . . . To be without these channels of global communication is self-defeating and weakens efforts to overcome Old World insularity.

—The commodities in the mobilia are for the use of all people. Use them enjoy them then leave them for others to enjoy. You can contribute things to the mobilia but you should not take anything away. If you wish to own an object do not keep it at the mobilia. The mobilia should not encourage private ownership. *My* house *my* stereo *my* telescope *my* land—this psychology of possessiveness must give way to *our* house *our* stereo *our* telescope *our* land . . . But even such joint ownership does not become petrified into any kind of exclusivity. Today *our* mobilia is shared with a fluid group of people tomorrow or next week or next month *our* mobilia will be another shared with another fluid group in another part of the community or planet.

—The private possession of people is even more reprehensible than the possession of objects. The mobilia must not accommodate the hording of people or of love. Love must be inclusive not exclusive.

At one time the individual who could not commit himself to a one-to-one relationship was considered neurotic. In our fluid times it is precisely the individual committed to an exclusive relationship who is immature.

Are you in love? Are you involved? Are you married? Whose man are you? Whose woman? Do you go with someone? These are all anti-universal. The Up-individual has many involvements many relationships many loves.

Once you have outgrown the primitive-childhood hangup of exclusive love you will find fluid love the more humanized.

Do not look for some one to love. Look for some *ones* to love.

To be in love with only one person is to be arrested at an infantile stage of parent fixation.

To be deeply involved with only one person is to thwart your potential for growth.

To be with the same person day after day is a bore.

—The private ownership of people and of goods cannot be overcome so long as the private ownership of children persists. To free the child we must not only do away with exclusive parenthood. We must also eliminate something far more basic—biological parenthood.

Creating a new life is too important a decision to leave to one individual or couple. The concept of individual rights in procreation is primitive. We need collective planning collective procreation collective child-rearing.

In our rapidly interdependent world the rights and welfare of humanity must not be subverted to the whims of individuals.

Not long ago people believed that it was their right to beat up their *own* wives and their *own* children. People also considered it their right to throw garbage on their *own* side of the river or lake. Hardly fifteen years ago birth control was denounced as an infringement on the right of the individual.

Moreover it is a delusion to believe that having a child is an assertion of your individual right. What individual right? What do you have to say about the mixture of genes that develops into a child? You want a girl you get a boy. You want a dark-haired dark-eyed child you get a blond blue-eyed one. You hope for a beautiful baby you get hit with a lulu. You cannot even determine its physiological intellectual and psychological dispositions. If you or your mate has recessive genes can you even be sure that your child will be free of inherited diseases? Or whether you will have a baby at all or have twins or triplets? Where then does your decision your so-called individual right come into all this?

The newborn is a product of chance. This is haphazard breeding—impersonal arbitrary.

But babies are not radishes to be produced haphazardly. Come let's have a child. No let's have three children. Let's have four. It is time we stopped treating human life as though it were a commodity produced by whim.

Human life is too precious to leave to chance. It is no longer enough to give children suitable environments *after* they are born. We must give each newborn a chance to start life with healthy genes. This is where the quality of each human life is first determined.

We must decrease the quantity and increase the quality of newborn life. (Every year several million babies are born with genetic defects. Fifty percent of all diseases are hereditary.)

How do we maximize collective participation in the creation of every newborn life? How do we go beyond slam-bang breeding and exclusive parenthood to universal-planned procreation?

—We must begin by rapidly spreading a new moral climate in the world de-romanticizing the whole archaic mythology of motherhood and fatherhood. Just as at one time procreation out of wedlock was stigmatized let us now attach a stigma to exclusive parenthood (private enterprise in children). If two people have a child do not shower them with congratulations and gifts. Congratulations for what? For their ego trip?

Let us stop romanticizing parenthood and make people fully aware why they really have children particularly in our times—

Having a child today is an act of supreme selfishness. It is the ultimate indulgence in narcissism.

Having children is a submission to cultural conditioning. Society has always expected young couples to have children—so they still obediently have children. When a woman says that she feels the urge within her to have children she is ascribing to biology what is nothing more than cultural programming. There is no such thing as a *biological drive* to reproduce.

Having children is a cop-out from life. The woman

unconsciously knows that by becoming a mother she will be excused from holding a job going out into the world or being involved in its problems. This is a convenient rationale for the woman who feels inadequate at finding fulfillment in professional intellectual or recreational outlets.

Having children acts as a shield against the world in yet another way. In these fluid times when you can no longer be sure of holding on to a husband or lover, a child provides some source of security or rootedness. Men come and go is the unconscious reasoning, they cannot be counted on. But here is the one love that is mine and mine only.

Having children means power. At one time economic and military power. Today psychological power. Here are helpless dependent lives you can control and manipulate. This is gratifying to a man or a woman with poor self-image.

Having children is considered a way of pegging down a marriage or an affair. Children have traditionally been viewed as adhesions holding relationships together. This doesn't work any longer. In our times children more often break up involvements.

These are *some* of the reasons people still feel driven to have children. At one time the reasons did not matter—now they do.

We must spread the awareness that people can now find fulfillment and love in new ways such as becoming involved in the Universal Family—the children and adults who are already here.

Instead of indulging yourself having a child indulge yourself by traveling.

Don't feed your narcissism. Feed the hungry of the world.

BEYOND FAMILY

You cannot guide others to defuse the population explosion if you yourself are fueling it.
The world is still full of unfed unhoused unloved children. They are now *your* children.

—To insure collective participation in the planning creating and rearing of newborn life every country must right away set up a *National Child Center.* (A few European countries already have.) These national centers must be coordinated with a *World Child Center* perhaps a modernized UNICEF.

—As individuals reach adolescence or early adulthood they must be encouraged—perhaps even required—to deposit their sperm or eggs and body cells at the National Child Center. Or at Sperm Banks Egg Banks Cell Banks supervised by the Child Center.

—At the Child Center a group of specialists comprised of geneticists biologists gynecologists social scientists and others diagnose each sex cell to determine its genetic condition and also study the psychological intellectual and physiological history of each donor and his/her ancestry. This group then advises which sperms and eggs are genetically best suited to produce new life. (The selected sex cells come from women and men of different ages different generations nationalities races physiological types. The donors themselves may now be dead or in their sixties or living far away. People are never informed whether or not their sex cells have been selected for reproduction.)

—At the Child Center another group comprised of demographers environmentalists social scientists and others with the help of computers regularly advises the rate at which the country and the world can comfortably accommodate newborn life. Based on these assessments a certain number of the selected sex cells are fertilized.

—The fertilized eggs are then implanted in the wombs of women who wish to carry babies and who have already been screened and approved by the *Genetic Counseling Service* at the Child Center. Later in the Middle Future fertilized eggs will be cultivated only in artificial wombs—under ideally controlled conditions to maximize the chances of creating the very healthiest babies. And to free women of the primitive ordeal of carrying babies for nine months. Still later stored body cells will also be carefully examined by Child Centers to decide which ones are best suited for cloning new life.

—The newborn spends the first five to ten years of its life at Child Center Homes. A *Universal Baby-Exchange Program* can enable babies to grow up at different Child Center Homes around the planet. Warm cheerful comfortable these Centers are open to men and women who wish to be with children. Every effort is made to provide children maximum opportunities to enjoy loving (but nonfixating) relationships with many women and men. To free the child and help it grow unpossessed and unpossessing it must be conditioned from its very first day out of the womb to develop a sense of security from non-exclusive relationships with *many* mothers and fathers. This pattern must then persist through childhood and adolescence. No child belongs to any one. All children belong to every one. Whose child are you? How many brothers and sisters do you have? How many children do you have? All these questions become irrelevant. You are everybody's child. Everybody's brother and sister. Everybody's parent.

—When the child is around eight or ten years old the Child Center places it in a mobilia and until the youngster is around the age of fifteen or sixteen the Centers continue to supervise its development facilitating the youngster's movements from one mobilia to another. Of course all this is done with the collaboration of the peoples within the various mobilias. The World Child Center also helps facilitate the youngster's movements around the planet.

—Thereafter the youngster is on its own. It can move around singly or trans-mobilia. This youngster does not belong to any specific parents specific family group or nation. This is a child of the world at home everywhere belonging to all humankind.

More than a century ago the Marxists launched a revolution to correct social-economic injustices. Today we are launching a more ambitious upheaval to redress the more basic biological injustices and monopolistic family systems which are at the root of social-economic wrongs.

Communal approaches to child-rearing in some

socialist states and the present trend to Day Care Centers in the United States do not correct basic flaws. Communality or multiple parenthood must begin in the pre-natal stage and persist full time throughout childhood.

We must jointly decide how many new lives the world can accommodate every week every month every year.

We must jointly participate in procreation by using our healthiest sex cells.

We must jointly be involved in child-rearing.

All this was not possible at one time. Today the Biological Revolution and the new mobility make all the above accessible.

We must settle for nothing less than—

Universal Planned Procreation.

Universal Child-rearing.

Universal Life.

Don't be a biological purist. Don't be a psychological monopolist.

Let every newborn have the best available genetic foundation.

Let every newborn belong biologically and socially to the whole world.

Only then can we end such primitive monopolies as my own mother my own father my own brother my own sister my own child my own people . . .

Only then can we end the destructiveness of exclusive love the fragmentation of our world into exclusive groups sects nations.

Only then will it be possible for all men and all women to be truly brothers and sisters.

beyond schools

universal
communication

The only way to modernize our educational systems is to do away with schools.

School is as obsolete as family.

Like the family, the school is inherently conservative insular structured. It reinforces many of the problems the individual faces at home—exclusivity competition fragmentation.

The school is a book-oriented system. It has no meaning in our electronic age.

The school system is oriented to a slower more

structured world. In our rapidly changing world by the time the youngster has graduated much of what he learned is outdated.

The school is predicated on the stability and continuity of the community. It has no place in our world which is increasingly fluid and discontinuous.

The school system cannot accommodate students who are on the move. They are considered bad students. Yet it is precisely the mobile who are now in pace with a world itself on the move.

All over the planet we are feverishly building more and more schools colleges universities. All along these schools are becoming superfluous.

A new *concept* of education is steadily replacing the school system.

Where is this new concept of education practiced? Where can it be found?

It can be found everywhere. It is all around you. It is called Universal Communication—travel television transistor radios satellitephones videophones films microfilms cassettes computers international publications tele-sessions tele-newspapers communication satellites encounter groups dialogue travel . . .

This *is* the new education. It is the fastest growing educational movement in the world.

Today's youngsters are more knowledgeable than youngsters ever before precisely because of Universal Communication. Not because of schools.

Schools are actually holding them back. Thwarting their potential for more rapid growth.

Education has become too big for classrooms and schools. We have outgrown the school system.

Education like family is developing into a Process—
unstructured spontaneous universal.
The whole planet is now a school.

But people still cannot acknowledge this new
concept of education. (Some reviewers and readers
were disturbed at my contention in *Optimism One*
that we do not need schools but more and more
communication satellites and travel.)
People are still fixated on the old assumption that
education is obtained in classrooms with teachers
pupils textbooks curriculums. Anything else is not
serious.
The concept of Universal Communication is
disturbing because it has no structure. After all where
are the schools? they ask. What are the curriculums?
What kind of degrees? Where do you all meet?
The same old story of craving structures. Here again
it is the fear of letting go of structures that slows down
progress.

In modern communities liberal educators still want
to *modernize* the school system. Give students more
autonomy, they urge, more voice in all school matters.
Deemphasize grades and exams. Do away with the
lecture system. Encourage informal open discussions.
Make use of teaching machines etc. . . .
These are considered progressive reforms. I don't
doubt that they improve the school system. But the
fact is that the system itself is inherently conceptually
unmodern and therefore these so-called progressive
reforms are relatively superficial—piecemeal measures.

In backward communities too valuable resources time energy are squandered building schools and emphasizing literacy—reading and writing.

Early-industrial countries have an obsession for building new schools. More and more and more schools.

Right-wing and Left-wing governments alike are caught in this school craze. Their officials proudly rattle off statistics on the number of new schools.

This is considered progressive leadership. It is presumed to be the surest and fastest way of making progress.

The fact is that these early-industrial countries are taking the *long* way to the future. In building schools they are feverishly adopting an *archaic* system.

Leaders and educators in early-industrial as well as in advanced-industrial communities are all dragging their feet. They are crawling into the future at a time when they could take giant leaps educating more people with less money less waste less effort.

Universal Communication offers a Big Push. In one neat sweep we can bypass innumerable problems— incompetent or inadequate teachers, student inequalities (in intelligence talent personality economic background) inadequate facilities, poor or outdated textbooks, competition, the tyranny of exams and grades, opportunistic attitudes to learning . . .

In the age of global travel communication and automated instant learning schools are an absurdity.

Rather than squander time money effort building schools, governments and educators must vigorously actuate the new potentials. Here is a guideline.

—Sponsor extensive education programs on television and radio.

One new school can educate only a few hundred students at a time.

One television channel can educate a whole country.

One satellite network a whole continent.

A couple of satellite networks all the people of our planet.

—Set up centralized computer systems enabling people anywhere to retrieve any information at anytime.

—Provide free or inexpensive education cassettes learning kits and other audio-visual aids to children and adults for Instant Education.

—Jet youngsters across the planet. Busing them across the city is no longer enough. Provide numerous travel grants for children. Set up Children Exchange Programs. Arrange travel projects for children to travel singly or in groups all over the planet.

—Tear down all school buildings. Set up instead instant *People Centers.* Cheerful modern transportable People Centers open day and night where people of all ages of all backgrounds from all parts of the planet can *freely* gather to meet talk play eat and drink discuss projects make use of facilities or just sit back and watch fellow people come and go. People

Centers will have microfilms cassettes videotapes. computer centers recording and broadcasting studios global communication facilities gymnasiums playrooms playgrounds gardens . . . People Centers complement the mobilia in facilitating the flow of people and ideas through the Universal Process.

—Technical training within the professional field itself. For example a medical student will obtain theoretical education from audio-visual recordings (microfilms cassettes etc.) and his specialized training at tele-medical centers. An astronomy student will obtain supervised training at an observatory and theoretical information through the programmed devices . . .

—You the Up-individual can do much to dismantle the school system and reinforce the trend toward UniCom—

—Get out of school college university.

—If you move trans-mobilias help free the children from schools.

—Having dropped out of the school trap you are now freer to tune into UniCom. Whether you move alone or trans-mobilia surround yourself with the most modern communication facilities. The more of these you have the more deeply you are involved in

BEYOND SCHOOLS

UniCom and the Universal Process. In opening up to the world you maximize opportunities to grow and become part of humankind. To use the old jargon— you are then an "excellent student" attending the "best school."

—Having dropped out of the school trap you are now also freer to organize discussion groups research projects play sessions encounter groups and so on. It makes no sense to sit stiffly in formal classrooms when you could meet more comfortably and intimately in a house a garden at a People Center on a beach on a ship—anywhere. Social interaction in school is unavoidably structured and regimented. You meet the same students the same teachers day in and day out for months even years. You all pursue a specific academic course with specific goals specific curriculum at specific times at a specific rate in a specific place. You can now achieve far greater intimacy variety spontaneity in social interactions meeting with whomever you please whenever and wherever. Social interaction is most meaningful when it is an open fluid process.

—Get out into the world. Just get out. The earlier in life the better. In insisting on class attendance the school system immobilizes the child at the very stage in life it could most benefit from travel. The earlier a child travels and lives in different cultures the better its chances of growing up fluid and universal.

If you want to condition a child to love its fellow people let it go out into the world and *meet* its fellow people. Let it *grow up* with them.

If you want to learn geography why languish in a classroom for months? Travel.

If you want to learn history and anthropology why not experience them directly—in museums ruins monuments in homes villages cities all over the planet?

If you want to study international affairs why not become involved in such affairs?

The more you travel the more involved you are in UniCom.

Make the whole planet your school. Every person you meet is your teacher every person your student.

—Having dropped out of the school trap you are now at last free to learn and grow at your own pace your own rhythm your own time. Through the use of learning kits cassettes computers and other automated instant devices you can now learn in a few hours or days what the school took months and years to cram down your throat. Why must it take a whole academic year to teach an intelligent person that the capital city of Poland is Warsaw or that dinosaurs at one time inhabited the earth? Why must a child who does not like arithmetic have to suffer through it when pocket calculators and mini computers can now do all his computations? Why must a child squander twelve years festering in classrooms cramming what it could learn far more leisurely and meaningfully with a learning kit and pocket TV traveling all over the planet? Why fritter away another four or seven or twelve years obtaining "higher education" which any intelligent person could more leisurely integrate in a year or two? Why thwart people's potentials for growth by encumbering them with irrelevant requirements, humiliating exams and degrees, emphasis on competition and opportunistic attitudes to learning, impersonal structures which make no allowances for individual aptitudes interests pace?

The whole school system is now too slow too static too structured. It is founded on outdated premises and values not in keeping with the rhythm and the spirit of our times.

Let us free our youngsters and ourselves from the tyranny of schools. Don't be afraid to let go. Hook into Universal Communication.

beyond industrialism
space age technology

Before the 1800s we had feudal technology—horse
carriages droshkies caravans gaslight sailing ships slave
and serf labor small towns villages town criers . . .

Since the middle 1800s industrial technology—
steam locomotives steamships electrical power
assembly-line production subways newspapers
telegrams radios telephones automobiles airplanes
cities . . .

Since the middle 1950s Space Age Technology.

We are now at the beginning of an epochal
technological transition.

Suddenly all around us the old industrial technology is falling apart. Advanced-industrial communities of Europe and the United States are suffering the full brunt of this breakdown.

Telegrams take days to reach their destination. Mail service is slow. Subways and trains are rundown and undependable. Electric power systems fail. Cars jam streets and highways polluting slowing down mobility maiming and killing people. The big cities themselves have become giant ghettoes—ugly dirty overcrowded filled with dingy rat-infested catacombs called apartments for which people pay exorbitant sums.

This is the collapse of an old decrepit nineteenth-century technology no longer suited to the needs the expectations and the rhythms of the late twentieth century.

We must rejoice in this collapse.

In urban communities however there is increasing clamor for *improvement* of technology. People want cars that do not pollute. Faster mail and telegram service. More fossil-fuel plants for uninterrupted electricity. Subways and trains that run on time . . . What they want is to shore up the old industrial technology.

They are like the people of the nineteenth century who wanted better stage-coach service cleaner droshkies brighter gaslights larger plowshares faster spinning wheels more nimble town criers. They too could not see the emergence of a new technology. They were content with improving the old.

Most urban dwellers today think along the same lines. They want to improve the old industrial technology.

This is a costly losing battle. This is patchwork.

You cannot regenerate a technology which is intrinsically obsolete.

Cars for instance were fine so long as there were only a few. But hundreds of thousands of cars jammed into city streets designed for horse-drawn carriages create basic problems which cannot be solved by simply producing non-polluting cars.

Fossil-fuel power plants (coal gas oil) were also adequate so long as urban communities were relatively small with modest electrical needs and so long as people lived in large family units collectively using a few electrical appliances. But today's metropolis is structurally dependent on massive electrical output. Then too our social systems are changing—millions of people now live alone in private dwellings each privately benefitting from more and more electrical appliances and gadgets. Such mammoth and mushrooming demand on electricity can no longer be met by simply building more conventional power plants.

It is all too obvious that we need new technologies —new sources of power new concepts of communication and transportation new concepts of economics new concepts of community.

Advanced-industrial societies however are confronted with two major obstacles to a massive shift to the new Space Age Technology.

1. The colossal problem of dismantling the old industrial technology and replacing it with the new. (I will discuss this a little later.)

2. Psychological and ideological resistances to new technologies. This is a very serious problem. In the big

cities of Western Europe and in particular the United States there is growing hostility to technology. Justified anger at the tottering old industrial technology is generalized into a whole philosophical resentment of all technology. Too often this resentment atrophies into a back-to-earth purism, a reactionary resistance to all progress.

In the U.S.A. some of what passes for conservation is nothing more than conservatism. There are strong reactionary tendencies among some conservationists which defeat the drive to clean and beautify the environment. Too often conservatism masquerades in the name of conservation. Under the currently fashionable banner of ecology some conservationists conveniently give vent to their traditional American doomsday hysteria.

This anti-technology mania particularly in the U.S. is nothing new. It is in keeping with an age-old pattern. **Those who cringe from progress have always resisted new technologies because new technologies invariably usher in radical changes.**

In the nineteenth century traditionalists ferociously resisted the railway system. Later they resisted the radio—intrusion into privacy, they protested.

The automobile? Why do you want to go faster?

The airplane? If the good lord wanted us to fly he would have given us wings. This has now been updated—if the good lord wanted us to fly jets he would not have given us propellers.

Every emerging technology every breakthrough precipitates resistances and exaggerated fears. People invariably fixate on the very worst possibilities completely ignoring the potential benefits.

We must be vigilant to make sure that new technologies work only for our betterment. Concern about our environment can be positive vigilance. But we must never allow this vigilance to atrophy into a resistance to progress.

Early-industrial countries face a different kind of problem. They are going berserk importing technology. But what technology are they importing?

The old industrial technology. Cars—more and more cars. Buses trains subways steamships fossil-fuel power plants urban sprawls . . .

They think they are modernizing. In their eagerness they are hurriedly encumbering themselves with an archaic nineteenth century technology.

This is as absurd as their efforts at cultural modernity. In their attempts to advance culturally leaders and intellectuals in developing countries are hurriedly building opera houses theaters symphony halls art galleries and buying up paintings. Suddenly it has become chic to go to the theater and to hang paintings all over the house.

They are feverishly aping old art forms deluding themselves that they are now modern.

Importing nineteenth century technology is of course far more serious. First because progress is slowed down. Second because in five or ten years these countries will be saddled with many of the problems now hounding the advanced-industrial communities pollution overburdened utility services clogged streets and highways automobile fatalities airport congestion urban decay.

Already many of these problems are beginning to be felt in the large urban centers of developing countries.

Early-industrial countries can take shortcuts to the future by embracing not the old industrial technology but the emerging Space Age Technology. Theirs is the advantage of not having first to dismantle the giant octopus of industrial technology. They can up-wing from the late feudal technology to the Space Age.

All nations advanced-industrial as well as early-industrial must make plans to move rapidly into the Space Age. Guideline—

—The United Nations must immediately set up a *Universal Technological Council.* This council must comprise technologists, communication and transportation engineers, city planners, architects, computerers, cybernetecists, sociologists, psychologists, economists, political scientists, environmentalists, visionary thinkers. *These Council members must be familiar with Space Age technology and enjoy reputations in their fields for vision and innovation.*

—Every country or regional bloc advanced-industrial as well as early-industrial must also immediately set up a *Technological Council.*

—If an early-industrial country or bloc does not have competent Space Age planners it can engage some from the Universal Technological Council (Unitec). Three or four Space Age planners can help establish a Technological Council in a developing area acquaint it with new trends catalyze it to new directions.

—The Universal Technological Council as well as the National and Regional Councils with the help of computers must then proceed to draw up plans. Farsighted projections of trends in the next ten twenty thirty forty years. For instance new techniques in procreation, the single life, the rise in universal-style mobilias, the increasing mobility fluidity leisure, the rise of multi-national corporations and regional blocs, universalism, space travel . . .

—Based on these and other projections the Technological Council must then draw up plans for applying the new technologies. This will call for Big Push mobilization. What are *some* of these Space Age Technologies for the Middle Future?

Transportation.
—Within communities: automated people movers, automated monorails, helicopters, solofly (better known as Pocket Pack now used in the U.S. and Canada for mountain hopping or flying across short distances).

—Hover-trains, hover-planes, hover-crafts, hover freights, hover boats, hover yachts—all using air cushion principle. Some hover vehicles already in use.

—Magnetic trains floating above magnetic tracks at 350 mph.

—Automated vehicles traveling in automated guideways within communities between communities across continents. You ride in a remote-controlled vehicle, dial your itinerary, central computer takes over and transports you safely to your destination . . . Meanwhile you sit back and rest read watch television . . .

—Helicopter buses, helicopter shuttles, helicopter patrols, helicopter ambulances, heli-movers, heli-deliveries, heli-visits on rooftops and gardens . . .

—Vertical take-off planes, short take-off and landing (STOL) planes . . .

—Supersonic and hypersonic planes. For long-distance travel. At present it is *possible* to travel from Paris to New York *door-to-door* in two hours. You helicopter from Paris to Orly. Supersonic across the ocean. Helicopter from Kennedy to New York City. You leave Paris at 5 P.M. arrive 1 P.M. New York time—arriving four hours *before* you left. Hypersonic planes projected for the late 1980s will zip you *anywhere* on the planet in less than forty minutes.

—Space shuttles projected for the late 1970s will ferry people between earth-moon, earth-space stations . . .

UP-WINGERS

Communication
—Pocket lasers, laser phones, pocket phones, videophones, satellitephones. These will help upheave inter-people communication and work patterns.

—Two-way TV, closed-circuit TV, frame-freeze TV, three-dimensional TV, tele-newspaper, international facsimile and photo transmission, international tele-medicine.

—TV patrols. These TV eyes already used in a few American cities will be placed at street junctures and intersections. You will turn on your TV set and watch activities in any community on the planet. Let's see what's going on at Trafalgar Square, let's watch the strollers on the People's Street in Peking, switch to Rome and see if the cafés on the Via Veneto are crowded . . .

—Portable computers. Already available and spreading. To communicate with individuals, retrieve information from Central Computer Services, take over housework shopping office work . . . Computer speech synthesizer reads to you from printed material.

—Central Computer Services. Accessible to anyone at any hour day or night by videophone satellitephone two-way TV or computsat to obtain or transmit information on very nearly anything. For instance weather conditions in any part of the planet. C.C.S. at

mobile medical centers will provide instant information
on a patient's background or provide quick diagnoses.
C.C.S. at national regional and U.N. headquarters will
hold instant referendums on community and universal
matters. C.C.S. will help minimize and in time
eliminate waste drudgery bureaucracy in government
in international and regional agencies in corporations
medical systems transportation systems agriculture . . .

—Communication Satellite networks. In the 1980s it
will be possible to reach very nearly every man
woman and child on the planet. And to hear from
anyone anywhere via satellitephone videophone
videolaser videosat computsat.

The above projections are illustrative showing only
some of the technologies in the coming years.
I repeat—we are at the beginning of an epochal
technological shift.
Space Age Technology is a new dimension in
human life. This is a technology that can reach the
moon in nine hours. Whip messages across the planet
in seconds. Make astronomical computations in
microseconds. Perform physical mental and
managerial tasks.
Space Age Technology is global—involving everyone
and every facet of life.
**Family marriage school full-time work
bureaucratic government city nation—these are all
feudal and industrial systems. They were viable so
long as we had feudal and industrial technologies.
These systems cannot and will not survive under
the emerging Space Age Technologies.**

**They are too structured too fragmented too slow
too rooted.**

**Space Age Technology will generate its own life
styles. Redo all aspects of life.**

Unfortunately the shift from the old technologies to
the Space Age is now advancing piecemeal and
uncoordinated. We are shuffling into the future. *good*

The result—decay pollution suffering archaic life
styles.

Our entire planet is now *conceptually* in the Space
Age. We urgently need visionary technological
councils visionary planning massive mobilization of
efforts and resources to up-wing swiftly to the marvels
of the Space Age.

beyond cities

instant
communities

What are the most beautiful cities in the world?

Paris Rome London Copenhagen San Francisco Rio de Janeiro—these are the cities most often mentioned.

Other favorites—Kyoto Bangkok Adelaide Jerusalem Cairo Athens Leningrad Budapest Vienna Venice New York City Mexico City . . .

We are all so thoroughly brainwashed by Old World values and esthetics that we absolutely cannot see the ugliness of all these cities. An ugliness which stares us in the face.

In fact the more dirty old and drab a city the more people seem to admire it.

But what the hell is so beautiful about Paris London or Vienna? What is so beautiful about tight dingy sunless streets . . . austere gloomy cathedrals . . . drab old buildings with dark cockroach-infested rooms and halls . . . decrepit old shops piled with junk . . . bleak factory buildings and decaying industrial neighborhoods?

We have been brainwashed to see beauty in ugliness, modernity in squalor, culture in oldness, esthetic charm in drabness and uniformity.

We fail to see that it is the people of the major cities who are relatively modern—not the cities themselves.

Let us not blame modern technology and progress for the breakdown and drabness of the big cities. These are not modern cities. They are all Old World.

Every single city on the face of this planet is now one massive garbage dump. Every single one of them.

In fact the ones we consider the most beautiful— Paris Vienna San Francisco—are among the ungainliest.

But so long as we go on believing that our cities are beautiful and holding up old rundown cities as models we will continue to fester in these mammoth garbage dumps.

It is absurd to complain of ghettoes when every single city is now little more than a large ghetto.

It is absurd to clamor for a better safer more civilized life as long as we continue to languish contentedly in these cities which are themselves intrinsically dehumanizing.

Governments can go on pouring out millions to renew or modernize the cities. They are only frittering away money time energy. These old cities cannot be rehabilitated. They cannot be modernized. Urban renewal is a colossal farce.

All our cities are obsolete. The very *concept* of city is obsolete.

London Paris New York are conceptually medieval cities. Built to accommodate horse carriages gaslights small neighborhood stores and family-oriented religion-oriented work-oriented feudal life.

Even our few twentieth century cities like Los Angeles and Brazilia are conceptually archaic because they too were built on premises of older technologies. All existing cities must go. They are all too backward and deficient too rooted in Old World values and economics in old technologies and obsolete institutions—churches temples and mosques castles and monuments streets and alleys schools factories prisons slaughterhouses cemeteries . . .

It is too costly and disruptive to tear down the cities and start off on the same sites with new concepts of community life.

We must begin by closing down whole areas of our cities (as the Chinese are now doing in Peking). Then within specified times close down the cities altogether.

We need not tear them down. Leave them intact as *Museum Cities* for tourists to visit and historians to study.

We speak of preserving historical landmarks in the cities. The cities themselves are now historical landmarks. We should leave them as they are—and get out.

Jerusalem Damascus Athens Paris London New York Tokyo and other old cities are historically too valuable to tear down. We need to preserve at least some of the cities.

At present in the name of modernization we are tearing down the cities bit by bit. The result is that we neither have Space Age life styles nor are we preserving the pristine condition of the cities.

Our cities are all too old to tear down too old to live in. They are now valuable only as museums.

Museums can be interesting to visit but not to live in.

We live in the Space Age and need Space Age concepts of collective life—spacious mobile instant cheerful global.

—Every country or regional bloc must right away set up at least one *Instant Community*. This can act as a catalyst to start a trend away from cities to new concepts of community.

—No attempts should be made to transform an existing city to an Instant Community. Space Age Communities must be planned and set up along new concepts and on new sites.

—The Instant Community must above all reflect and accommodate the new mobility. An entire community of over 100,000 people can now be set up in less than six months. It can stand for a few months or years then the whole community may be dismantled or moved. A trend has started toward mobile homes and communities. For example in 1972 nearly fifty percent of new housing in the United States comprised mobile homes. Tent cities mobile cities Disneylands— these are forerunners of Instant Communities. Rapidly assembled their emphasis is on movement and fun. Most blueprints of future communities are based on Old World premises of permanence and rootedness. This is the central error in these projections. They do not take into account the exploding mobility of people and social systems.

—The Instant Community must therefore incorporate only the newest concepts of construction. This means no stones bricks steel or concrete. No foundations. Nothing static permanent or rooted. Nothing that will stay long enough to decay corrode or degenerate into ghettoes and tenements.

—The Instant Community must have only Instant Habitations. Light sturdy colorful habitations made of aluminum fiberglass plexiglass plastic and other modern synthetics. These Instant Homes are highly flexible and maneuverable. Press a button and you rotate the entire house, tilt it to different angles to catch sunlight or moonlight, make it crawl float on water or fly. These Instant Habitations have great variety in design color and shape. They can be flown ready-made or packaged by helicopter to desired sites, easily assembled easily enlarged and just as quickly dismantled or transplanted. Bubble houses can also be instantly packed unpacked inflated to house people then deflated and packed up again.

—The Instant Community must combine the most beautiful aspects of nature with the technology and life styles of the Space Age.

—The Instant Community can be set up in a green valley a desert near a mountain on a lake or sea— whatever topography is desired. Even outer space.

—Some of our Space Age Communities will actually be in Space. Our present space stations will soon evolve to huge Cosmograds (Astrovilles). Within a few years hundreds of men and women will occupy Space Communities and Lunar Colonies. At present space engineers space architects space scientists are planning these extraterrestrial communities. Some of the concepts designs and materials could be used in our Instant Communities here on Earth.

—The Instant Community must enjoy the freedom of controlled weather. Bubble domes can be moved around to protect parts of the community from rain snow or scorching sun. For instance if people are at the beach why allow a sudden downpour to ruin the fun? If the clouds cannot be conveniently dispersed float the transparent bubble dome overhead. At a later stage communities will also benefit from solar and lunar satellites to turn on instant sunshine sunlight at any time night or day. We will regulate the weather in our communities as easily as we now regulate the temperature in our homes.

BEYOND CITIES

—The Instant Community will be extensively automated and therefore dependent on abundant electric energy. Mobile nonpolluting Nuplexes (nuclear energy complex) situated outside the community or on floating platforms can provide abundant cheap energy. The Nuplex will not only meet all the electrical needs of the community, it will also provide power for the cybernated agriculture and industry, help recycle wastes, desalinate water . . . Later in the Middle Future the community will benefit from solar energy.

—The Instant Community must insure ample elbow room. Congestion leads to environmental decay social pressures violence. I am not sympathetic to the concept of the megalopolis or mile-high skyscraper cities. They perpetuate the old problems of congestion and asphalt environments. The Instant Community I am proposing does not and must not throw people on top of one another. Space Age transportation and communication are upheaving our concepts of distance. People can have ample elbow room ample open space and greenery without feeling isolated. Hop into your helicopter or the automated monorail and you will visit friends in another community a hundred miles away more quickly than it now takes to visit friends across the city.

—The Instant Community must only benefit from Space Age transportation systems. This means no cars buses trucks or subways. Streets are obsolete. Only modular automated transportation—people-movers monocabs monorails . . . Also extensive airborne transportation—solofly hovercrafts helicopters . . .

People will assemble not on streets but in
public gardens mobilias People Centers playgrounds
beaches . . .

—The Instant Community must accommodate the
ceaseless flow of people. Therefore numerous
attractive heliports shuttleports stolports hoverports in
and around the community. These will have cafés
hotels TV centers computer centers . . . People will fly
in from faraway communities and continents hold
meetings here have rendezvous luncheon then fly out.

—The Instant Community must also be linked up
with global communication.

—The Instant Community is Universal. The sense
of community exists not only within the community
but more and more within the whole planet. The
individual does not belong to a specific community
but is part of many communities—part of the whole
planet.

—The Instant Community must be turned on to
Space Age concepts of art. Not simply new styles of
art. But new *concepts* of art. This means no operas
ballets theaters art galleries or paintings. (Those who
wish to view this old art can visit the old Museum
Cities.) New concepts of art may comprise
Sky-illuminations—variations of gigantic colorful
designs projected against day or night skies. Graceful
movements of people and objects under weightless

conditions. Stimulation of the pleasure centers of the brain enabling the individual to achieve sublime visions hallucinations ecstasies. Headgears for electronic music from anywhere on the planet or pulsar beats from the galaxies. Multi dimensional films and holograms. Live video views of our sculpture-space-ships gliding across the heavens. Home screens and giant outdoor screens hooked to space-station telescopes providing the most celestial shows of all—kaleidoscopic spectacles of the Universe with its ever-changing galaxies and super-novas brilliant suns and star clusters trail-blazing comets and asteroids . . . Space Age art like Space Age philosophy will continue to grow more and more cosmic and transcendent. The artist is now as obsolete as the priest. The artists of the new age are primarily the scientists and visionaries who strive for transcendence to new dimensions of Time and Space.

—The Instant Community must include extensive opportunities for fun and play. Bubble-dome playgrounds and swimming ponds. All-weather convertible athletic fields. No violent spectacles such as boxing wrestling bull-fighting American football. These spectacles perpetuate pseudomasculine glorification of brute force. People who enjoy watching such brutalities are as sick as the gladiators who engage in them. Instant Communities must also disallow competition in sports. No tournaments matches contests. Why do we need to know who the fastest human is? Or who the strongest? Or who the best tennis player? Any jackass can run faster. Any dumb bull is stronger. People who play to win want to exercise their egos—not their bodies. Sports should emphasize fun not rivalry. We need no scores no winners no losers no medals. Only the reward of getting together to play—the joy of play.

—The Instant Community must not accommodate Old World institutions which perpetuate violence and harbor death. Prisons must give way to rehabilitation centers. Slaughterhouses must give way to nonviolent eating habits—eating meat is an act of violence. Cemeteries must give way to Immortality Centers which as I will later explain will help perpetuate life through longevity hibernation temporary suspension or other methods.

—The Instant Community must be extensively cybernated. Computerized housework and officework. Universalized education. Tele-medicine. Agro-industrial complexes. Long-distance TV shopping day and night. Automated transportation round the clock. This means no cumbersome hospitals schools shops department stores farms. This also means less and less bureaucracy less and less work. The Instant Community must be strongly oriented to leisure mobility fun.

—The Instant Community must benefit from Space Age concepts of government. Bureaucratic government representative government democracy political parties elections—these are archaic concepts of government. The Space Age process of government is by Instant Universal Referendum. When necessary central computers hold community and global referendums then automatically act on the consensus. Those who fail to instant-communicate their views are reached automatically. Central computers instantly activate a receiver-device on their videophone videosat or pocket computer and request their opinion. Central computers can reach or be reached by anyone anywhere anytime.

Today we have the resources and the ability to set up our first Instant Communities. In creating such total Space Age environments we will evolve beyond the decaying old cities set up catalysts to prod us more rapidly to new patterns of wholesome universal life.

beyond survival economics

cybernated world of leisure and abundance

The people of Planet Earth work too hard.

We spend nearly two-thirds of our lives working. Earning a living and doing housework. We feel impelled to work even on vacation.

We are all so thoroughly programmed by millenniums of struggle for survival that though we no longer need to struggle we still go on struggling.

Our economic systems work habits cultural values all arise out of the age-old struggle for survival. Feudalism capitalism socialism are all survival economics.

Modern capitalism and socialism are still survival-oriented work-oriented hardship-oriented guilt-driven.

They are still impaled on the hard-work mystique.

In most countries around the world there is growing unemployment. Every year hundreds of thousands of high school and college graduates join the unemployed. How are capitalist and socialist governments coping with this rising problem? They are struggling to provide jobs. More and more jobs. Capitalism and socialism have a mania for jobs.

The Soviet Union and the United States have sophisticated automation on the moon and on space stations performing complex tasks which would take thousands of people to accomplish. Yet here on Earth they still abide by the old economics of finding jobs for people.

Not only are our economic systems archaic. Our cultural values are backward too. We need not only new economic systems but also new values new attitudes to work and possessions to leisure and pleasure.

Socialism and capitalism are hopelessly predicated on puritan values. Work hard study hard produce produce. You must work—work work work. Hardship and hard work are good for you. They will help you grow. They will help your country grow . . .

So insidious is this brainwashing that people cannot relax even on their vacations. Are you having fun here on the beach? Not really. I feel I am wasting my vacation. I haven't read a single book. I haven't had meaningful conversation with anyone. I haven't even done any of the work I brought with me from the office. I have wasted my whole vacation.

The new economics is not capitalism or socialism or even the new mixture of the two. The new economics is the new technology— Automation Computerization Cybernation.

The only relevant economists of our Space Age are the automaters computerers cyberneticists. They are the economists of Leisure and Abundance.

Cybernation (computerized automation) is an entirely new direction for humankind. It is a major technological upheaval. The cybernated system combines mental organizational and physical work. The new cybernated system makes decisions and produces. If it breaks down it repairs itself. If it makes a mistake it corrects itself. It even reprograms itself.

The Russians have that spunky Lunokhod on the moon—hiking, climbing mountains, going down hills, scooping up rocks, taking pictures, relaying films, measuring distances, recording moonquakes, sleeping during lunar nights, waking up for the lunar days, communicating with earth, occasionally pausing to repair itself and so on. Soon Marsokhods and Planetkhods will be performing even more complex chores on the more difficult terrains of Mars and other planets.

This very day we could have such cybernated systems doing much of our work here on earth as well.

In developing fields such as the space program world tourism airlines world transportation international hotel services credit card systems construction off-track betting fewer and fewer people are handling more and more work through extensive computerization. This technology could be used in many other fields—the development of unlimited solar

energy, the production of unlimited synthetic foods
and miracle crops . . .

**If we mobilized this new technology we could
within ten or fifteen years do away with poverty in
the world.**

**If we mobilized our new technology we could
within five to ten years free millions of people rich
and poor alike from the slavery of perpetual work.**

This all sounds too good to be true. Enough to make
any Right-winger or Left-winger shudder with guilt
feelings. I don't see doctrinaire capitalist or socialist
economists bucking the hangups of centuries to
embark on the new economics of Leisure and
Abundance.

In fact socialism and capitalism the two major
economic systems of our times do not even have the
ideological frameworks to cybernate their entire
economies.

Cybernation is an outgrowth of modern technology.
Not of socialism or capitalism. The Soviet and United
States governments are only now hurriedly embarking
on crash programs to make way for computers.
Neither government has yet formulated long-range
plans for massive cybernation. Cybernation is
spreading *in spite of* socialism and capitalism.

—Capitalist and socialist governments in
advanced-industrial and early-industrial countries must
right away set up *Leisure and Abundance Councils*
comprised primarily of computerers cyberneticists
visionary economists and social scientists to formulate
rapid universal application of automation and

cybernation. Such a total shift from the old economics to the new will entail entirely new formulations on employment productivity income budget work habits leisure.

—Early-industrial economies—capitalist and socialist —are focused on industrialization. This is now a long slow route—not a shortcut to the future. These backward economies can now take giant leaps forward by avoiding industrialism embarking instead on a massive program of automation computerization and cybernation.

—Socialism and capitalism are still fixated on eliminating unemployment. No economic measures no crash programs can any longer reverse the global trend toward unemployment. Nothing can any longer be done to replace the jobs which automation and cybernation are steadily taking over. It has become an economic imperative to decrease work. This is not only sound economics it is also a humanizing move. **This is a time to free people of work. Rather than rack their brains to create employment economists should now work out plans to create leisure.**
Unemployment is no longer the problem. Employment is now the problem. We have the technology to do our work. Free the people so they can grow as humans rather than as working-machines.

—Cybernation means not only less and less work but also greater freedom within work. Through the use of computers sattelitephones telex facsimile tele-conferences two-way TV frame-freeze TV closed-circuit TV videophones people can now do more and more of their work directly from home beach or jet. It is less necessary to emphasize rigid work schedules or rigid office attendance. Do not commute to work—communicate with work.

—Cybernated economies also lead to the steady obsolescence of cash-money and the rapid emergence of credit systems. Automated-magnetized-global-credit-systems enable the individual or the corporation to make small or extensive transactions anywhere on the planet without transferring or even carrying any cash at all.

—Cybernation also accelerates the rise of multinational corporations and multinational staffs.

—The waning of national economies and the continued development of regional continental and universal economies.

—The emergence of regional and eventually universal currency units. As the trend toward regional blocs multinational corporations global tourism and world trade accelerates there will be increasing pressure as in Western Europe today to create a unified currency system.

—Cybernated economies also spread abundance based not on exclusive possession but on temporary usage. People need not own but briefly rent houses gardens villas yachts helicopters hovercrafts computers . . . When they stay at a mobilia they enjoy all existing commodities (as in resort hotels today) then leave them for others to enjoy.

—Cybernation will spread abundance without significant redistribution of wealth. Karl Marx a visionary in his times could not have envisioned the monumental breakthroughs of this late twentieth century. His followers today still call for the redistribution of wealth. This is Old World reasoning. We no longer need to redistribute anything. We need to develop the limitless energies and resources now suddenly opening up to us—fusion and thermal energy, endless solar energy, phytotrons, agro-industrial Nuplexes, ocean-bed farming, which can produce unlimited quantities of hybrid crops and synthetic foods and goods . . .

—You the Up-Winger can do much to help the trend to the new world of Leisure and Abundance—

—Don't work your life away. Live. If you work more than three or four days a week four or five hours a day you are dissipating your life. Not playing enough not living enough not growing.

Leisure is creative. Playing or doing nothing are a part of growth. Laziness can be good for you.

People who work eight hours a day five days a week year after year decade after decade are automatons. They may advance professionally but hardly evolve as humans. Whole areas of their minds and personalities remain stunted. They are one-dimensional.

But I enjoy my work, you say. The point is that if all you enjoy is your work you are limiting your experiences and enjoyments. Your life is still one-dimensional.

Leisure-work plans now being considered—

Four-day workweek.

Three-day workweek.

Seven days on seven days off.

Month on month off.

Six months on six months off . . .

The new demand should no longer be we want jobs. Rather WE WANT LEISURE. More and more LEISURE.

—Don't submit to the tyranny of rigid work hours. Westerners have made a virtue of punctuality promptness efficiency. These are qualities we should expect of our machines. Not of people. Cultures that emphasize promptness and efficiency are tyrannical. People who are punctual and efficient are Dangerous. They have been reduced to robots.

Rebel against the tyranny of having to drag your corpse out of bed at an *exact* hour every morning (at that hour it is a corpse) arriving at work at *exactly* the same hour leaving at *exactly* the same hour day after day year after year. Such precision is an assault on your humanhood.

—Don't hold on to a job. Move. Be fluid. If you have been at the same job more than two or three years get out. You are not contributing to your firm's development or to your own growth. You are vegetating. Long-term commitment to a job or even to a career is part of the slow structured Old World. In our fluid age it is a sure sign of the static personality.

—Between jobs take long vacations—weeks months if possible years. Leisure travel fun are creative. They help the human in you.

—Work at firms of different nationalities preferably in different communities and countries. In becoming involved in international economics you will help the trend toward universalism and yourself grow universal.

—It is not enough for governments to work out new cybernated economic systems, we need new values. You yourself must want and demand more leisure more flexible work schedules more mobility. You yourself must want to break away from the puritan mystique of hard work.

—The relaxation and humanization of our primitive work habits will not in any way limit our drive to higher standards of living. On the contrary we can now quantum-leap into a world of Abundance

BEYOND SURVIVAL ECONOMICS

Creativity Leisure by working less and letting our efficient tireless machines do the work.

Fewer and fewer people working less and less can now produce more and more and more. This is the meaning of the new cybernated world of Leisure and Abundance.

beyond nations

the planetary movement

For the very first time in history we have the
beginning of a global movement. This movement is
daily gaining momentum. It will continue to spread till
it has touched every human life.

It is no accident that last month in your community
students asserted their new expectations. Last week it
spread to the workers yesterday the women today a
minority group tomorrow the prison inmates then the
soldiers then the clergy the trans-sexuals the
consumers . . .

It is also no accident that last week people asserted
their rights in Tokyo yesterday in Ankara today in

Mexico City tomorrow in Cairo then in Manila then in Rome then in Jerusalem then in . . .

No one can any longer thwart this planetary movement as it spreads from one profession to another from one city and continent to another.

At one time it took years and decades for a movement to extend from one country to another. Today global communication whips it across the planet in hours days weeks.

Even more directly the people of the world are now helping one another as never before.

Swedes and Norwegians helping build villages in the Middle East . . . Chinese fighting tropical diseases in Zanzibar . . . American youths helping build roads in Brazil and Afghanistan . . . Danes and Peruvians teaching school in the United States . . . Israeli technicians and agronomists helping out in West Africa . . . Egyptians teaching at schools in Libya Sudan and Kuwait . . . Russians building dams in Egypt . . .

United Nations technicians all over the planet fighting malnutrition and disease building hospitals and houses distributing milk and birth-control devices . . .

For humanitarian reasons for political and economic reasons for whatever reasons—the people of this planet are cooperating and helping one another as never before.

The major issues of our times are no longer national —but global. Peace economic progress population explosion poverty pollution disease world tourism satellite communication global transportation weather modification space . . .

These and other realities have suddenly interconnected humanity. There is no escaping it.

These realities involve all humanity and must be tackled by all.

Our awareness is also growing increasingly universal. Today as never before we *know* of conditions around the planet. We can no longer rationalize poverty or romanticize backwardness. We can no longer look the other way pretending that problems elsewhere do not exist or are no concern of ours.

The problems are numerous complex global. But our means for dealing with these problems are also growing more and more numerous effective and global.

How can you the Up-Winger be an effective participant in this spreading planetary movement?

—Begin by *consciously* disavowing your nationality.

You have outgrown religion. You must now outgrow nationality.

What is your nationality?

I am Universal.

But where are you from?

I am from Planet Earth. I am Universal.

In refusing to identify with a country you are taking the first conscious public stand against nationality. You are identifying with all humankind.

In emphasizing your new global identity you are helping its psychological and intellectual impact to grow on you and on others. You are spreading the new awareness.

You are also compelling people to relate to you not

as a member of a separate artificial bloc—but as a
fellow human.

—Organize a People's Movement and petition the
United Nations to initiate a new status—*Universal
citizenship.* This is our planet. It no longer makes
sense to draw lines and say this is my territory the
other is yours. This is no better than the urine borders
charted by dogs.

From here on we recognize no national borders. All
countries now belong to all peoples of this planet. No
government has the right to bar anyone from leaving
or entering any territory. **To place restrictions on our
freedom of movement is a violation of our human
rights.** Passports visas exit permits residency rights—
all these formalize restrictions on our freedom of
movement across this planet which now belongs to all
of us.

—Reject all claims to "internal affairs." We must
not regard any nation's affairs as exclusively internal or
domestic. We want more and more involvement in
internal affairs of other nations. This is our planet—
anything occurring anywhere is everybody's affair.

—If you are studying languages you are wasting
your time. Not contributing to the planetary
movement. National languages are inoperative in our
converging world. French German Spanish Arabic
Hebrew Swahili Urdu—all these are dying languages.
All national languages are on their way out. We are
moving toward a Universal Language.

Today English and Chinese approximate universality.
English has distinct advantages. It is the language of
international relations modern technology world trade.
It is spoken on all continents and is relatively easy to
learn. In the next three or four decades English will
serve as the universal language—*Unilang*.

(This Unilang itself is transitional. For a glimpse of
future computer language listen to the astronauts: ALL
GO ON CSM . . . EVA NEXT . . . 90 SECONDS TO LPD . . .
OVER . . .) It's now Go on Unilang.

—Common markets regional blocs international
agencies multinational corporations—all these are
movements away from nationalism and fragmentation.
They are steps in the right direction. They help expand
communication dialogue trade interinvolvement. On
all continents there are now strong movements toward
regional cooperation. These multinational ventures
need support.

Above all get behind the United Nations and its
subsidiary agencies. For centuries people have been
dreaming of a world government. Now that at last we
have the beginning of one what are you doing about
it? If you are doing nothing you have no moral right to
complain about its shortcomings. Did you expect this
world body to start off full-grown and blemishless?

The United Nations is *your* world government. It is
your own government—not simply your country's.
You must become *personally* involved in it. The U.N.
charter begins *We the Peoples of the United Nations*
. . . The Peoples—not the governments.

Your national government is after its own petty
national interests. That is why the United Nations has
had difficulties. For you the Up-Winger your

government is the United Nations. You must deal directly with your world government helping and strengthening it.

—Modern technology is the Up-Winger's greatest ally. Without it the planetary movement wouldn't have a chance. Space Age communication and transportation is helping humanize and universalize us. It is unifying the people of our planet as no force has in the past.

In December 1970 seven men were sentenced to death in the Soviet Union and six others doomed in Spain. World public opinion rallied to their defense and saved them from execution. There could have been no world public pressure without universal communication.

On April 30, 1970 the president of the United States announced his country's invasion of Cambodia. Within hours all hell broke loose. Mass demonstrations strikes rallies protests shootings riots. They spread like wildfire across the country then across the planet— London Stockholm Tel-Aviv New Delhi Tokyo Melbourne . . . In the United States over four hundred colleges closed down. University presidents and faculties housewives businessmen laborers veterans joined several hundred thousand others to converge on Washington. The New York *Times* reported that the stock market "came close to a full collapse not on the news that the war might end, but that it might lead to major escalation." The outrage continued to grow and boom and explode . . . Exactly eight days later on May 8 the president was forced to go on television to announce the sudden decision to end the invasion.

As far as I know never in our entire history had the people of the world ever rallied as universally and successfully to put an end to an injustice. This world pressure would not have been possible without global communication.

Universal Communication is our unsung instrument for Peace.

UniCom works for the people far more than for governments. UniCom has suddenly exposed governments to public view rendering them highly vulnerable to national and international public opinion.

UniCom is providing a powerful platform for dissent. It is coordinating and unifying dissent— linking up the people of the planet. I repeat it is not an accident that movements now spread quickly from one profession or group to another from one city to another from one country and continent to another.

UniCom is inherently beyond the control of governments and groups. If a government controls the press and the mass media the world still comes tumbling through by way of foreign publications foreign radio films television people on the move. UniCom cannot be censored or shut off.

As UniCom grows more powerful the people grow more powerful. As UniCom grows more universal people grow more universal.

The weaker mass communication within a country the weaker the people the stronger the government.

The stronger mass communication within a country the stronger the people the more vulnerable the government.

In technologically advanced countries like the

United States individuals who appear every night on national television wield more influence than government leaders.

We are now farther away from Orwell's 1984 than ever in the past. To sink into a 1984 world of Big Brother authoritarianism entails dismantling our entire global communication and transportation systems. This is no longer possible. Modern technology is our greatest safeguard against bleak Orwellian projections.

These are some of the new realities of universal communication which elude Right-wingers and Left-wingers still bogged down in Old World attitudes to technology.

Up-Wingers regard UniCom their strongest ally.

To be effective in the planetary movement you must be extensively linked up with UniCom.

—Join the planetary convergence—Travel.

Travel means communication—direct human communication. You must use modern transportation systems to move around the planet and *be the medium* through whom different cultures link up and communicate through whom barriers are brought down dialogue circulated interinvolvement generated . . .

"People are very good for each other," writes Richard Farson the psychologist. "We need intimate relationships of long or short duration, to remind us of our membership in the human race, to help us be less afraid of one another, to permit us to laugh and cry with one another."

Travel enables us to do all this. It enables us the peoples of this planet to shake hands with one another to touch and to feel and to experience firsthand the humanness of one another.

To travel is to be involved in the planetary movement. Anyone who travels is automatically an activist. Anyone who travels.

To travel is to infiltrate to influence to participate in domestic affairs of communities to pose alternatives to local conditions. Even passive tourists by simply moving around infiltrate. The village child sees them going through and thinks "I want to be like that woman. I want to be like that man." You have planted the seeds of unrest. This infiltration is partly nonverbal. The very presence of strangers acts as a catalyst for consciousness-raising, a human link with the world outside—a world of new possibilities and potentials.

Millions of tourists pouring into a country year after year themselves become a movement for change. Tourists have already started upheavals all over the planet. This is why reactionary regimes try to discourage tourism in their countries.

Do not boycott countries whose governments you oppose. Those are precisely the lands to frequent. In boycotting a country you boycott and isolate its people weaken the channels of global communication strengthen the government and perpetuate the status quo.

—The greatest movements today are outside politics. The most progressive changes take place in spite of governments. The planetary movement is for the most part beyond the scope of national governments.

Political leaders as a rule are driven by personal

ambition too involved in problems of day-to-day housekeeping too boxed-in to traditional Right-wing and Left-wing philosophies too vulnerable to the whims of the conservative masses to initiate or actuate far-ranging goals.

Politics is no longer the most effective way to change the world. Governments are developing into managerial agencies which run the everyday affairs of cities and nations. As I explained earlier computers can now manage these affairs of state more efficiently. In time computers will replace governments.

This tradition of relying on the government to do things—like a Papa—is Old World.

Don't waste your anger on lackluster leaders. Use your energies more constructively. "No use trying the government controls everything." This is a cop-out.

Gone are the days when the government controlled everything. In today's open fluid world the government is only one of many forces influencing events. Global communication for example is a far more powerful force generating its own pace and momentum radicalizing and diversifying all our institutions values life styles.

Many of the greatest upheavals today take place outside government—the biological upheaval the women's liberation the sexual liberation the environmental movement the consumer uprising the information explosion the planetary convergence . . .

No government can any longer reverse or even impede the cumulative impact of these and other peoples' movements. Today the individual is more powerful than ever. The individual has communication facilities mobility information knowledge awareness. These are powerful tools.

Organize your own Up-Wing movements. Help start Cell Banks Mobilias People Centers Instant Communities. Start a movement for a three-day work week or a six-month work year. Rent helicopters to swoop down on faraway communities and bring medicine information. Help mount a crash movement to attain immortality . . .

Rally public support. Remember that world public opinion is daily growing into a powerful force. That governments are increasingly vulnerable to public pressure. That movements today can spread faster and deeper than ever before. "Pressure from the people alone shapes world history" says Chou En-lai. This has never been more true than today.

—The planetary movement is totally committed to *life*. There is no cause no goal no ideal worth dying for. Nothing is worth your life. If any movement jeopardizes your life—forget it. Try another way. If anyone exhorts you to any kind of violence get away from him. He is not an Up-Winger but part of the old spirit the old tactics the old masochistic death-oriented philosophies and revolutions. The Up-Winger is totally nonviolent totally committed to life. To the Up-Winger **Life itself is the greatest Revolution.**

part 3

the cosmic upheaval

The cosmic upheaval is an entirely new event on
Planet Earth, a new dimension in human existence.

Today we are witnessing the very beginning of an
upheaval that is altering our basic human situation.
This cosmic dimension supersedes all our past
aspirations all our past philosophies struggles
revolutions.

There has never been anything like this on our
planet or probably in this whole solar system.

The cosmic upheaval is not simply a historic event.
This is a major evolutionary perturbation.

Historically we have already made impressive

progress. As I attempted to show in *Optimism One* in modern communities we have more freedom more equality more individuality more communication more integration more love more fluidity more control over the impositions of nature more humanness than ever before in our past.

Psychologically socially economically politically we have made monumental progress through the ages. We are moving up and up from the abyss.

This descendant of fish this child of recent monkeys has done well for itself.

But great as these advances are the basic human situation itself has changed very little. Our advances have been historic not evolutionary.

The human condition remains inherently tragic.

To free humanity from this tragic plight and rise to a higher evolution we need a new kind of upheaval—a cosmic upheaval.

We can no longer settle for traditional revolutions which seek to improve our social economic political conditions. That is no longer enough.

Revolutions and revolutionaries are now too modest. We want more. Much more.

We are now far more visionary far more demanding far more transcendent.

Progress itself is no longer enough. It took us ages to even accept the idea of progress. Now we must adjust to the idea of cosmic changes.

We must begin to adjust to the idea of making *basic* changes in the human condition—for instance redoing the human body, going to other worlds, living extraterrestrially, experiencing a different nature, searching for other beings in the universe . . .

We must begin to comprehend that living in other worlds and living eternally are no longer metaphysical or theological concepts. People are now actually traveling to other worlds people are now actually striving for physical immortality.

When we speak of hearing voices from other worlds we no longer mean the voice of a god—but of astronauts.

When we speak of people leaving this earth we no longer mean that they have died—but that they have gone to other planets.

We are moving into whole new dimensions of Time and Space.

We must therefore begin to embrace the idea that from here on our goals are not only social economic political. That at last the time has come for humanity to tackle more primary problems strive for more transcendent goals.

We must make every man and woman on this planet aware that we are now at the beginning of a monumental upheaval against the twin limitations of Time and Space, that it is only by joining and sustaining this upheaval that we will at last free ourselves from our human tragedy.

We must make everyone aware that Time and Space are the most basic determinants of all life impinging on all aspects of life—from birth to death. They are the root causes of the deepest human suffering—unfreedom robotization inequalities competitiveness violence loneliness identity crisis alienation . . .

Parent-child conflicts sexual inequalities social injustices economic imbalances political repressions—these are not the primary determinants of human suffering. They are

**contributory causes themselves created by the
twin pressures of Time and Space.** This is a truism
which all too often eludes us.

How do the limitations of Time and Space (Biology
and Environment) account for our plight?

BEYOND FREEDOM

Let us begin with freedom. What does freedom mean
to you?

The psychologically oriented will emphasize
emotional or inner freedom. The doctrinaire socialist
or capitalist sees freedom in an exclusively economic
context. The political determinist regards freedom as a
political condition. A sophisticated generalist is aware
of all these aspects of freedom—psychological
economic political.

What does repression mean to you?

Here again the psycho-social economic political
determinants are invariably stressed.

We are all so totally focused on social economic
political conditions that we never pause to consider
freedom and repression in a more basic human
context.

We are like the shipboard passenger vehemently
demanding a better cabin or the freedom to stroll on
the first-class deck—on a sinking ship.

The ship of your life—your very existence—is
slowly sinking. No psychological economic or political
freedom can save you from drowning. It is time you
paused to consider this.

What good social freedoms when life itself is based
on unfreedom?

How free am I if I cannot choose my own body my
own brain my own sex the color of my skin my

biological life style? How free am I trapped in a predetermined biological strait-jacket in whose selection I have had absolutely nothing to say?

I do not like my body. I am unattractive chubby clumsy sickly. What can I do about this body of mine? I am trapped.

I do not like my mind. I am slow unimaginative unperceptive. How can I free my self of this mind?

I do not like my personality. I am disposed to depression paranoia intolerance. I wish I were different. How can I free myself?

I am growing old. My hair is turning gray my eyes are losing their luster my mind and memory are fading. I don't like what is happening to me. I don't like myself any more—this aging self of mine. I am a burden to myself. How can I now recapture my earlier vitality? How can I slow down Time?

What good then social economic political freedoms if I cannot enjoy the more primary freedom to free my self from the prison cell of this unwanted body personality brain? How free if I cannot decide if I cannot even know when I will die? What does freedom mean to a terminal patient? In one blow death strikes down all freedoms. Death is Zero freedom.

Then too how free am I within a Space-cell which determines and limits my every move—gravity air water nature seasons night and day the sun? What good freedom to move all over the planet if a mere twelve-foot fall can kill me? What good freedom to sail the open seas if a pint of water in my lungs can drown me?

I am an accident—a biological accident trapped in a very small speck in Time and Space. I am a momentary flash of consciousness. Suddenly I am. Then just as suddenly I am not.

All my attempts at psychological economic political self-determination are child's play. They will not bring me *real* freedom. They will not set me free.

BEYOND THE HUMAN ROBOT

Alarmists contend that mass technology and mass society are robotizing the modern individual. They speak of the programmed individual depersonalized mechanical.

In *Optimism One* I explained that modern technology is actually helping us grow less machine-like less programmed less manipulated.

Yet notwithstanding our social gains all people modern and primitive alike are intrinsically programmed. The animal-human organism itself is structurally a robot. A rigid robot manipulated by its predetermined biology and environment.

What is more robot-like than having at regular intervals to inhale and exhale to eat drink urinate evacuate sleep? All these mechanical functions are programmed into me. I have nothing to say about them. They are beyond my control.

If I stopped breathing for only a few minutes—a few quick nothing minutes—that's it. If I don't eat or drink or sleep at regular intervals my body begins to flounder my mind begins to go fuzzy. Last night in the middle of a deep merciful sleep I suddenly jumped up robot-like and rushed to the bathroom. There I was in the middle of sleep half-conscious half-alive holding my thing.

Is there anything more programmed more manipulated than all this? Yet we take it all for granted call it human even romanticize it.

In modern communities there is now much talk about the individual's right over its own body particularly in such matters as sex abortion drugs etc. . . . But what rights over your own body? You enjoy no real rights no control over your own body. Try telling your body not to breathe for a few minutes. Try not relieving yourself when the pressure builds. Your body is not manipulated by you. You are manipulated by your body.

Then too we are helpless robots manipulated by environment. I once traveled on a malfunctioning train. A sudden power failure shut off the air conditioner. Most of us took off our jackets. Then the lights suddenly went off. Soon we all fell off to sleep. Then suddenly the lights went on again. We all sat up again reading and talking. Then the air conditioner went on and we all put on our jackets again. During the next few hours each time the lights went on we sat up and read. When the lights went off we obediently fell off to sleep. When the air conditioner went on we quickly put on our jackets. When it went off our jackets came off.

There we were like marionettes manipulated by a crazy power system.

Is this not precisely the condition of our existence? Day breaks we wake up, night comes we sleep, the cold sends us scurrying away for cover, then the heat then the cold then the rain . . .

What do you or I have to say about all this? Is there a manipulation more arbitrary than that of environment which without any consultation with me or you decides the seasons the heat of the summer the cold of winter the cycles of night and day light and darkness decides when it will rain or shine when it will unleash a hurricane or an earthquake?

COSMIC UPHEAVAL

Every year around the planet tens of thousands of people perish in floods fires heat waves cold waves snowstorms typhoons cyclones hurricanes earthquakes and many other arbitrary manipulations.

Even a simple picnic or sports event enthusiastically planned in advance must be forfeited at the last minute because the sky has suddenly decided to piss on our heads.

The very people who rebel against manipulations by a political regime or an economic system obediently even cheerfully accept the more repressive manipulations of biology and environment. "Why do you want to make genetic alterations in the human body or implant electrodes?" protests a radical political activist. "What is wrong with the body as it is? Why fight death? When my time comes I'll go. Why control the environment? It is more exciting not to know when it will rain or snow or shine. I like the variety of seasons anyway."

But what variety? Variety imposed by environment not by you.

People obediently accept such basic manipulations yet invest energy and time even their lives fighting human-made institutions which in relatively superficial ways manipulate them.

There is no government no industrial-military complex no economic system no mass media which can ever reduce us to puppets and robots as the biological and environmental dictatorships have.

BEYOND EQUAL RIGHTS

What does equality mean to you?

Equality you will say means *feeling* equal. It means

having equal social and political rights. Or equality derives from a just distribution of wealth.

We can continue gaining these equalities—social sexual economic political—but so long as there is no *biological* equality there can be no real equality.

Biology is the primary perpetrator of inequality. People are *born* unequal. Not simply dissimilar—that is not bad. But unequal.

The literature and folklore of all societies are crowded with themes dramatizing this most primary of inequalities. The bright attractive child favored by everyone over its brothers and sisters.

The beautiful peasant girl discovered by the prince and taken to the palace to be his queen. Too bad for all the homely girls who have to stay behind in mud huts.

The tall handsome man spotted by Mr. Rich Man's daughter. The hell with all the short skinny boys.

The brilliant individual who wins awards and the adoration of the whole country. Nothing for all the dum-dums who struggle year after year but can never go far as musicians writers scientists lawyers etc.

And what about the birds with broken wings—those born crippled blind deaf . . .

If all this is not inequality and injustice—what is?

So long as some are *born* healthy others sickly some strong others weak some bright others dumb some beautiful others ungainly some cheerful others gloomy some vigorous others frail—in other words so long as these gross biological inequalities persist there can be no real equality only the perpetuation of rivalries jealousies conflicts . . .

BEYOND COMPETITION

Run run run run. Where am I running? Why am I running?

I run not simply because my competitive family life competitive school system competitive economic setup have conditioned me to run. I run because of a far more powerful pressure—the pressure of Time.

I run essentially because my Time is limited.

Every day every hour every minute every second I am a little older a little weaker a little closer to the end.

Is there any social system any social pressure more competitive more dehumanizing than this biological pressure?

What time is it? It is five thirty. It is getting late.

Late for what? How can five thirty ever be late?

The fact is that it is getting late. It is always getting late. Even when I am resting it is getting late. Even then Time is running and compelling me to run with it. My life is running—out.

This is ultimately what we mean when we say it is getting late.

The running and competition are built into me—into my biological system.

No person on this planet is ultimately in competition with me. Everyone is finally running the same race against Time.

This Time-tension this race to the finish has nothing to do with East or West capitalism or socialism democracy or dictatorship technology or pretechnology. This is a universal dilemma.

You can remove modern technology remove watches and clocks and rigid work schedules—still the Time-tension will persist. The most insidious schedule is the rigid schedule of limited lifetime. The most brutal clock is the biological clock within my system ticking away and nothing anyone can do to stop it. This is surely the most brutal race of all.

"Drink for tomorrow you die." This was written long before modern technology and clocks long before capitalism and socialism . . .

Our competitive social economic systems only *aggravate* the biological race against Time. Not until we have defused the Time-bomb, the imminence of death, will we stop running.

Only then will Time cease to matter only then will all competition and pressure become superfluous. For why run then? You can take your time. You have all the time ahead of you. It will *never* be late.

BEYOND VIOLENCE

As I explained in *Optimism One* there is a historical trend toward nonviolence. Between parents and children between men and women teachers and pupils employers and employees leaders and citizens society and the criminal society and the emotionally troubled between nations between races between sects even between people and animals—at all levels of all societies there is a steady diminution in violence.

But there is still much violence in the world. It is no longer enough to focus only on the social economic political causes of violence. If we succeeded in removing these pressures there would still be violence.

Violence is inherent to our situation in Time and Space. The human organism is under relentless pressures from biological conditions within it and environmental forces outside it which at every instant threaten its safety its very existence.

Conceived in the precarious environment of the womb the human organism is then violently thrust out into an even more hostile environment outside. Left suddenly alone very alone. Threatened at first by light and noise and movements and the pressures within its own body. This human organism then goes through life forever exposed and vulnerable at the mercy of all kinds of violence—the violence of pain the violence of disease the violence of hunger and thirst the violence of abrupt separation from loved ones the violence of burning and falling and freezing . . . One misstep and we break a limb or crush a bone one misstep and we drown or choke or . . .

So perpetual are these violent threats within us and around us that we take them for granted and do not consciously realize that we are perpetually warding them off perpetually exposed and vulnerable.

Life is a relentless struggle against the violence of suffering and the violence of death.

This lifelong struggle makes us deeply insecure and suspicious disposing us to violence toward one another. It is curious that we are not more violent.

Not until we have remade—completely remade— the biological makeup of the human organism can we overcome our vulnerability to the ever-present threats of biological and environmental violence.

BEYOND HUMAN LONELINESS

Today we enjoy more individuality and at the same time more communication than ever before. We have had a long hard climb from the valley of hostile tribalisms and are now nearing summits of individuality and global communication.

Yet we look around and realize that our individuality and our ability to communicate globally are still not the answer. We are still lonely isolated separate.

We communicate better than ever. But how do we really communicate? We still have to communicate as separate entities. We still have to go through a maze of protective shells which every individual in understandable protection of its self has had to construct. We have to go through countless other protective layers which the individual in its anguish and anxieties has had to build to protect itself not only from the world but to protect itself from itself.

How then can I ever reach you really communicate with you? How can you ever really communicate with me—the inner me the real me? The me I myself dare not know cannot know.

How can you and I even when resting side by side and feeling close ever bridge the isolation which our separate biologies compel? No love no friendship no empathy no sympathy can fuse this separateness which is predicated on our separate minds our separate emotions our separate bodies.

There is a loneliness which no social system no individuality no communalism can allay. This is the loneliness which is inherent in our physiological separateness.

Loneliness is not essentially a psychological or social problem. It is rather a biological reality.

So long as we are separate biological entities there will be loneliness. So long as we are separate self-interest is unavoidable. Self-interest is chauvinism—self-chauvinism which is at the very root of all later chauvinisms and conflicts of interest.

BEYOND ALL IDENTITIES

The modern individual is now fluid and mobile as never before. He no longer belongs to a fixed family tribe or village no longer is committed to a lifelong profession to a religion nationality political movement philosophy of life. The modern no longer has a fixed identity. He derives a sense of selfhood and security not from total permanent commitments but from a sense of motion and continual growth. Nonidentity is the new emancipation.

But the individual is basically as immobilized as ever within fixed *biological* identities.

What are these fixed identities? They are this specific body of mine which I have inherited and cannot alter my inherited skin color my inherited sex inherited brain partially inherited personality.

How fluid am I compelled to remain pegged to these static biological identities which determine my very existence?

The real identity crisis today arises from my growing reluctance to accept my inherited biology. I refuse to be immobilized in predetermined biological identities in whose selection I had absolutely nothing to say.

Why should I accept this particular body of mine? Why not different bodies different sizes different shapes different colors? Why know only this specific sex? Why not the other sex or an alternation between both sexes or a fusion of the two sexes? Why accept this particular brain or this particular personality?

Why go through a lifetime trapped within the same body the same mind the same personality? What a bore. Future-people will look back and wonder how an individual could have gone through an entire lifetime with its one and only self.

I may be fortunate and have a graceful body a warm self-confident personality a vibrant mind. Still I am caught in a monotony a fixity.

Who at times has not grown monotonous to his own self? Only the rooted accepts his biological status quo. Only the static individual is content—or is it resigned?—to go through life pegged to inherited identities.

The dynamic fluid individual wants biological diversity biological emancipation.

He does not want only to be himself. That is too static too rooted. He wants the option to be also Andreas and Miriam and Emiliano and Yoshiku and Awolowowo and Jamileh and Stanley and Silvana and Sadruddin and . . .

He wants to maximize his fluidity not simply by merging and demerging with different people but also having different kinds and shapes of bodies different colors and designs different admixtures of personalities and brains the option to plug into human-machine systems and be such systems.

This is the biological freedom and fluidity we are finally striving for.

BEYOND ALIENATION

In February 1971 a severe earthquake jolted Los Angeles. Around fifty people died in that earthquake. The psychological damage was even more widespread affecting many thousands of people.

For weeks and months following the earthquake psychotherapists treated people suffering from earthquake jitters. Children were afraid to leave their parents. People young and old were gripped with profound anxieties emotional exhaustion depression inability to concentrate and to sleep nightmares . . .

Los Angeles psychotherapists* provided some of the common causes of the widespread emotional crises—

The unexpectedness of the quake.

The fact that there is no place to hide.

The feeling of complete helplessness.

The sense of having been betrayed by mother nature which people had always viewed as reliable and good.

The sudden realization that no one can finally save you. That parents friends mates leader types are themselves vulnerable and afraid.

A loss of confidence in the world.

The realization that one cannot predict one's own future. That ultimately there is no control.

The sudden reality of the tenuousness of existence— all existence.

These were some of the causes of the widespread psychological damage. Yet several months after the earthquake life in Los Angeles was back to normal. People were out of their shells having fun playing starting careers having children building homes planning for the future.

Has the threat of earthquakes suddenly disappeared? No.

How then do the people cope with their exposedness? They cope by *repressing*. They repress their anxieties and fears of more earthquakes.

Convulsing a whole modern city the earthquake was like a gigantic flash of self-illumination. One fleeting terrifying glimpse at the real human situation. The earthquake and its aftermath compressed within it the whole dilemma of human existence.

---

*Quoted in *Time* magazine, February 1971.

Life itself is an endless cycle of tremors and the ever-present threat of one final quake which snuffs out each individual life. People the world over suffer from "earthquake jitters." We *all* harbor horrendous anxieties—the unexpectedness of death. The fact that there is no place to hide. The feeling of complete helplessness—exposedness. The realization that no one —no parent friend lover or leader—can finally do anything. The inability to predict our own future. The desperate tenuousness of existence.

How do we cope with these cosmic anxieties? We cope simply by repressing. By refusing to face our real human situation. We run away from ourselves and from the world.

This is the real alienation. The root of all human alienation.

How can it be otherwise? How can I not feel alienated from my own temporary self which at any moment may slip away into permanent nonexistence? How can I help feeling alienated from my own fragile vulnerable body which brings me suffering— toothaches agonizing stomach aches throbbing headaches broken limbs? How can I not feel alienated from the world which at any instant can forfeit my existence? It is not only the ever-present threat of my own sudden extinction which precipitates this alienation but also the fact that people dear to me have died and others will at any moment suddenly die.

How then can I ever stop running away from my self and the real world? To face my self—to really face my self and the real world—is to face the fact that I am a highly vulnerable fleeting consciousness exposed to hostile forces over which I have no control.

I have stressed these problems in their rock-bottom elemental context to prod you to focus on our human situation. I am not surfacing these problems to depress you or simply to throw up my arms. This tract is not an exercise in metaphysical despair. Not at all. This is a tract for Action.

I want to energize you to action precisely because now at last our tragic human situation can be and must be reversed.

Until this stage in history we have run away from these fundamentals. They have been too tragic and we too helpless.

At best we rationalized them through theologic fantasies and philosophic speculations. Our attention and energies have been focused instead on immediate social economic political problems. In other words unable to do anything about our sinking ship we have quarreled over cabin rights and household chores.

The time has now come for us to confront our fundamental human situation. We now have the potential to overcome the basic tragedies and limitations.

But first we must *dare* to think and act cosmically. We must *dare* to want to overcome.

We must never again be resigned to the human condition.

Never again resigned to suffering. **All suffering is wasteful and diminishes the human.**

To think and act cosmically means to proceed from entirely new premises aim for entirely new goals.

Socialism capitalism democracy psychotherapy—all these deal with housekeeping chores. They have no answers to our fundamental situation no transcendent programs.

Psychotherapy can help allay some social loneliness but can it in any way allay the more basic biological loneliness?

Socialism can help reduce economic inequalities but can it in any way reduce the more insidious injustices of inherited inequalities?

Democracy can help reduce social alienation but can it in any way reduce the more basic alienation from our fragile bodies and terminal existences?

Even the planetary movement I outlined earlier in this tract is finally a dead end. It cannot reverse our basic situation.

We need a new concept of revolution a new concept of progress. A Cosmic Upheaval.

We need Visionaries Up-Wingers to launch this Upheaval. To bring this Time-Space dimension into the open.

This emerging potential to transcend our situation is the basis for the new Optimism. I am optimistic because I am supremely confident that if we mobilized our enormous resources we could around the end of this twentieth century up-wing to a higher evolution—become free in Time and Space.

How do we mount this Upheaval? How do we overcome the limitations of our human condition?

As I have already reminded you the two basic determinants of life—all animal-human life—are Time and Space (Biology and Environment). So long as we are at the mercy of these twin forces the human

condition will remain tragic—Time-bound and
Space-bound.

Our Cosmic Upheaval therefore must be aimed at
these two primary forces. We must free ourselves
within them by extending ourselves through them.

This Upheaval then is comprised of two fronts—
Space and Time (Environment and Biology).

THE SPACE DIMENSION

How do we defuse the pressures of the environment?
How do we break out of the limitations of Space?

—1972 will be remembered as the year
Earth-people established the first world environmental
monitoring system . . . United Nations Conference on
the Human Environment comprised of 114 countries
met at Stockholm issued an international declaration
on the Human Environment . . . Set up the *United
Nations Environmental Agency* . . . Headquarters
Nairobi . . . U.N.E.A. now creating *Earth Watch*—the
first worldwide system for monitoring the quality of
this planet's atmosphere soil and oceans. A global
system interconnecting satellites and at least 110
ground stations . . .

In 1972 *Earth Resources Technology Satellite
(ERTS-1)* sent into neo-space orbit around the earth
. . . ERTS-1 is the first of an up-coming generation of
permanent satellites for environmental monitoring . . .
This satellite's sensing devices now scan every part of
this planet's surface . . . It is relaying 200 billion bits
of information on the environment every single day
. . . This information is passed on to all nations
through the United Nations . . . In addition to

information on agriculture forestry geology metallurgy oceanography this satellite provides a constant flow of information on the global weather and environment—

Helps predict drought and soil conditions.

Helps predict volcanic eruptions and earthquakes.

Helps predict potentially destructive floods and storms.

Measures growth and decline of glaciers.

Shows snow levels.

Measures precipitation soil moisture and wind action (all helping prevent forest fires).

Scans the oceans which cover 71 percent of this planet and where much of the earth's weather is formed.

Helps provide accurate global long-range weather forecasting.

Space stations and Sky Labs provide additional monitoring and earth-scanning experiments. Then too supercomputers ten times more powerful than today's most sophisticated computers are now being designed to predict *broader* climatic changes years and perhaps even decades in advance.

All these projects will not only continue to help us forecast weather and predict natural disasters. What is infinitely more important they will help in our ongoing efforts to *modify* the weather and actually *prevent* natural disasters.

Experiments are now advancing in weather modification—We have had some success in cloud seeding to produce or increase rain, some success in cloud growth and fog dispersal, some control of hailstorms, some small dissipation of hurricanes . . .

International conferences are studying ways to predict weaken and prevent earthquakes . . . The Soviet Union has devised a quake-alert system . . .

Plans are developing to establish national and international agencies for collecting and regularly updating all seismic information . . . Lasers and other seismic detecting instruments are now in use in some areas of the world to measure earth pressures . . . More are planned more are urgently needed . . . Plans are also under consideration for injecting fluids or arranging underground nuclear explosions to weaken and even to prevent earthquakes.

Discussions and projects are developing on Controlled or Total Environments as protection from the rapacities of nature . . . The use of artificial moons or satellites to control tides and floods . . . Extensive weather changes through nuclear projects to alter cold ocean currents dam straits melt some icebergs etc. . . .

Weather forecasting and modification though still in its infancy is already helping save tens of thousands of lives every year and diminishing damage to crops and property . . . For instance it is estimated that were it not for an early satellite warning Hurricane Camille would have killed over 50,000 people in the United States in 1969.

But nature is still terrorizing life on this planet— floods fires earthquakes hailstorms tidal waves hurricanes tornadoes typhoons . . . We must stop this carnage. Every single decade several million humans die in such disasters. We must learn to regulate the weather in our communities and across the entire planet just as easily as with the turn of a dial we now regulate the temperature in our homes stadiums shopping malls.

—We must also learn to manipulate natural cycles— seasons, night and day—instead of being manipulated by them. *We* must decide what kind of seasons we want in what order and frequency. We must also have the freedom to decide the cycles of day and night rather than be programmed by their arbitrariness. We will continue to extend our influences over these cycles as we become less and less dependent on agriculture and develop new technologies.

We must launch a global program orbiting solar satellites to relay sunlight and sunshine any time night or day. An entire community or parts of a community can turn on instant daylight or sunshine at any hour the way we now turn on electricity or communication satellites. These solar satellites will enable us also to control the *degree* of daylight or darkness. If for instance we want everyone on the continent or on the planet to participate in some event such as a global referendum or a global holiday we can turn on daylight over the whole planet.

—We must launch a crash program to green the entire planet. At present we occupy less than one-fifth of our planet's *land* mass. For ages we have been barred from vast hostile areas of this planet. Even the friendlier areas we inhabit have shoved and pushed us around mauled and crushed and drowned and buried us at will. The violence of animals and humans is ample evidence of the cruelties of the environment.

Thanks to modern technology we are now turning deserts jungles ice continents into habitable areas. The Russians have diverted the course of a gigantic river to reclaim vast steppes, the Dutch have reclaimed extensive lands from the sea, the Israelis have converted deserts into gardens, others have *created* islands lakes rivers hills . . . Multinational explorations of the oceans are now going on with the intention of establishing extensive undersea communities.

The *United Nations Environmental Agency* must undertake a crash program to study and plan extensive geological changes and global gardening to transform the entire planet from the brutal jungle it has been to a friendly beautiful paradise.

—It is not enough to redo the planet. We must extend ourselves *beyond* this planet. **To limit ourselves to this infinitesimal speck in space is to limit our potential for cosmic growth. To transcend to a higher evolution we must transcend our earth-habitat.**

We have already taken the first steps. We are at the beginning of the Space Age. We have repeatedly visited the moon, sent space crafts to Venus Mars Jupiter and into interstellar space, are planning tours to the outer planets, have already set up space stations and more are planned. In the coming years hundreds then thousands of people will live outside this planet— on lunar colonies and on space stations. Still later we will inhabit other planets other solar systems and galaxies . . .

In transcending to new dimensions in Space we are transcending to new dimensions of existence.

Precisely because of its magnitude many people have had difficulty comprehending the Space dimension. Unable to cope they rationalize—We should spend the money on more important things. Why do we want to go out there anyway? And so on.

The protests are understandable. It takes relatively strong psyches to accept a perturbation of such magnitude. It also takes imagination.

The fact is that the Space Breakthrough is revolutionizing every aspect of life here on Earth. All our social medical educational economic political national systems, our technologies life styles philosophies self-image—all are shifting massively to the Space Age.

Directly or indirectly every aspect of human life is benefitting from the Space Breakthrough.

Nevertheless the resistances will persist for a while. In a way this is an old story. Through the ages the more timid of our species have always warned against moving out and up to new stages. First it was—

Don't leave the cave.

Then—Don't leave the tribe.

Don't leave the home.

Don't leave the village.

Don't leave the homeland.

Now—Don't leave the planet.

Another reason compounding these resistances is that people think of Space as dark and cold. This is chiefly because Space is most conspicuous at night when we can see the moon the stars the galaxies. Space is therefore darkness and darkness frightening. Of course darkness need not be frightening. When we have overcome our primitive fears of darkness we will find great security mystery and beauty in darkness. Moreover as we continue moving out into Space we will develop the ability to see through darkness more easily than we now see in daylight. Darkness will be irrelevant. Finally Space is not all darkness and cold. There are suns in the universe billions of times larger than our small sun. Regions in the universe brighter and more congenial than our solar neighborhood. Areas in the universe that never know darkness, bathed in perpetual sunlight and galaxy light of

COSMIC UPHEAVAL

fantastic brilliance and beautiful colors the like of which we do not have here.

If you are terrified of the darkness think of Space by visualizing the clearest brightest sky.

THE TIME DIMENSION

Of the two-pronged Upheaval against our primary human limitations the Time (Biological) Dimension is the more immediately important. In altering the human biology we alter our situation in Space setting the human organism free.

From here on we must work toward an entirely new concept of the human.

We must redo the human.

To redo the human we must begin by redoing the human body.

The body has been our greatest hangup. Our most serious obstacle to a higher evolution.

Too helpless to do anything about our primitive body we have brainwashed ourselves to regard it as a marvelous invention of nature. Biological purists and other traditionalists even romanticize the human body.

They are content with very little.

They refuse to see the human body as it really is—a primitive mechanism inherited from our animal origins, defective fragile limited perishable.

Even the most powerful young man is highly fragile. A prick of a pin makes him bleed. A wrong step and he falls breaking his leg. A blow on the head and the whole robust body collapses.

One hundred and twenty boys and girls playing happily in a dance hall are suddenly trapped in a fire and burn to death.

Three hundred thousand men women and children drown in a tidal wave.

Yesterday at a summer resort five young people were frolicking in the surf. Suddenly one of them drowned. One moment he was a human being full of life and laughter. Minutes later he was reduced to nothing—a lifeless mass of flesh.

I know a beautiful eighty-year-old man full of vision and hope. In spirit and idealism he is as youthful as the most dynamic youngster. Yet his body is old and withering. One day soon his body will die of old age dragging down with it his youthful mind and spirit . . .

All this makes no sense. It makes no sense at all.

We must rebel against the vulnerability of the human body.

We are all too exposed too fragile. At any instant we may be crippled or maimed for life. At any instant we may suddenly cease to exist.

We all go through life on the edge of a precipice. One misstep—just one misstep—and we cease to exist forever.

It is outrageous that such a beautiful phenomenon as life should be encased in such a fragile thing as the body.

Life is now too precious too full of fantastic potentials to be at the mercy of such a precarious thing as our primitive body.

Is all this a negation of the human body?

Yes. Absolutely yes. I am negating this animal-human body. This body so programmed and robot-like. This body so alone and unfree. So susceptible to pain and violence. This body so fragile and vulnerable.

My spirit—this human spirit of mine—soars into the heavens free unprogrammed unafraid reaching out to all my fellow humans reaching out into infinity and eternity—but this body of mine Space-bound and Time-bound drags it back.

Why then accept this limited body? So long as we are confined to our archaic bodies we will remain trapped at a primitive level of evolution.

We must not accept the human body. Never again be content with it.

We must modify the body redesign and redo it completely.

We must de-animalize ourselves.

We did not choose our body. We had nothing to say about it. It has been *imposed* on us by evolution itself influenced by the hostile environment.

But we can now remake the human body into something beautiful varied fluid durable. Into something expressing our new visions.

The human body is now obsolete. We already have human-made systems which can do very nearly everything that the body can do. Soon we will even reproduce human life outside the body.

Except for the human brain everything having to do with the body is primitive—belonging to the animal stage in our evolution. Eating drinking defecating reproducing sleeping walking dying—all these are pre-human.

The body itself has hardly changed in the last two or three million years. Only the human mind has been evolving.

I am no longer my body. This body is simply a physical extension of me. The organs in my body the flesh the liquid the waste the limbs and bones—all these are becoming incidental to my existence. They are all part of the animal-me the primitive-me. At one time indispensable to my survival they are now increasingly superfluous.

Only my mind has transcended the animal. My mind alone is exclusively human. My body is part of the Past my mind alone part of the Future.

Perhaps the Future will divide human evolution into two major ages.

Age One: The animal-human stage at which life was encased in animal-human body and therefore governed by the laws of nature and of Time and Space.

Age Two: The post-animal stage at which humans evolved beyond the animal-human and therefore Free in Time and in Space.

We are now reaching the end of Age One and beginning to move into Age Two.

We have already begun to alter the human body. The body is no longer what purists imagine it to be.

How are we beginning to redo the human body? What are some of the emerging potentials for more extensive biological changes?

—Reconstructive Plastic Surgery. Through such surgery we are now making extensive permanent physiological changes. We are altering the architecture of the head—face-lifts and hair transplants, redesigned eyes ears noses lips; reshaped cheekbones jaws chins;

obliterated wrinkles blemishes clefts. Plastic surgeons are also performing extensive body sculpture—breast augmentation and reduction stomach tightening thigh trimming recontouring of the buttocks redoing the shape of feet.

Sex-alterations are leading to increased trans-sexuality. Penises and testicles are now constructed or removed vaginas and breasts created or removed hysterectomies performed.

It is estimated that in the United States alone every year nearly one million people undergo cosmetic or prosthetic surgery. Such reconstructions and reshapings of face and body and sex are also spreading fast in Europe Asia Latin America and elsewhere.

Plastic surgeons are confident that in the Near Future they will be able to make more total changes such as redoing the entire size and shape of the body redoing the whole face altering the color of skin . . .

As we make more extensive changes biological identity will have less and less meaning. How tall are you? What is your race? Your sex? The color of your skin and hair? All these become irrelevant. You are trans-racial trans-sexual trans physical.

How old are you? That too is irrelevant. I was born fifty-two years ago. My new face is four years old. My hairpiece two years old. My kidney eighteen months. My Dacron arteries seven months . . .

—Genetic Engineering. Every day the mysteries of the human cell are decoded, the DNA created, techniques developed for genetic surgery gene manipulation gene grafting gene switching gene deletion. All with the help of lasers chemicals viral insertions . . . Such extensive genetic interventions will not only enable us to correct genetic or hereditary problems. What is infinitely more transcendent they will enable us for the first time to *create* entirely new kinds and forms and shapes of human life.

Biologists geneticists space scientists are now discussing and planning the creation of new mutants— people with larger heads to accommodate larger brains. Smaller bodies for greater adaptability. Slower aging processes. Legless bodies protruding eyes or other modifications for space travel and extraterrestrial colonization. Skins with different colors patterns and designs. Grafted or implanted membranes enabling the individual to live under water and to fly. Superhumans with genetically programmed knowledge superior intelligences and bodies etc. . . .

Such projections are valuable. For one thing they prod people away from biological traditionalism. They help generate a new awareness of our emerging potentials.

We need to involve more and more people in this Biological Upheaval so we can *jointly* decide what genetic modifications and improvements we desire and need. Having always been creatures of evolution we are now becoming the creators. To make wise biological decisions we need to be well-informed and well-involved.

—The Cyborg (human-machine life). We are also evolving from the animal-human to the human-machine. This is a gigantic evolutionary leap. The animal-human is at the mercy of evolution. The human-machine is created by human intelligence. The animal-human is terrorized by nature limited by Time and Space. The human-machine will transcend nature and evolve through Time and Space.

We are in the age of the cyborg. Individuals with Dacron heart valves transistorized pacemakers electronic limbs electronic bladders artificial kidneys silicone breasts contact lenses porcelain teeth . . . Then too individuals with ear phones attached to their heads walking around listening to music or voices from faraway sources.

We also have machines robots teleoperators computers automated and cybernated systems performing more and more human functions—mental managerial and physical.

This is only a beginning. The fusion of the human and the machine is gaining momentum. We will shed more and more of our animal organs and incorporate more and more human-created replacements.

Will all this lead to artificial people? Absolutely not. All this is leading to human-created people. **The more we humans remake our bodies the more human we will grow.** We have been pre-human.

I trust the cumulative wisdom of humans far more than the slow arbitrary workings of evolution.

Are the millions of people who wear contact lenses or have new teeth or breasts—artificial? When does a person become artificial? What if you wear a hearing aid and have new teeth then suddenly need a new kidney to keep you alive and later need new heart valves and still later some bone replacements—should we let you die or give you new parts to help you enjoy an active life? When should we stop helping afraid that you might become artificial?

What is so sacrosanct about this so-called natural body that we should leave it untouched? What is so beautiful about our animal liver or kidney—or any blob of flesh or piece of skin? A horse's ass is also skin. What is so romantic about defecating? Or so sound about this natural structure that is a fire hazard heavily polluted poorly ventilated badly insulated and handicapped with countless other structural defects. Any student of architecture knows that it is not even esthetic to place the playground so close to the sewer.

The hell with this natural body which is little more than a robot—a bad robot—limited gawky temporary. It is our animal-human body that is now artificial. It cannot even keep up with our human visions and dreams. **We ourselves can create far more versatile durable beautiful bodies.**

Let us encourage the present trend toward de-animalizing our bodies. Replacing our animal organs with human-created parts. Let us *all* become involved in planning radical improvements in our primitive bodies.

Let us for instance improve on our eyes not simply by implanting contact lenses but also micro-lasers micro-radars and sonars enabling us to see through objects through darkness and fog and across vast distances.

Let us improve on our ears not simply by implanting miniature hearing aids but also miniature antennas which can tune in to voices and sounds from anywhere on this planet and from far away in outer space.

Let us dispense with our stomachs and intestines to implant instead a miniature laser or TV connected to satellite stations so we can instant-communicate with anyone anywhere. Communication—not food—will be the nourishment of future-people.

Let us dispense with our lungs and graft instead gills and implant anti-gravity flappers helping us trans-live in the oceans and in the air. Walking is primitive. Future-life will be Space-free. We will fly and glide and soar . . .

Let us implant electrodes under the skin so we can better self-control our minds emotions bodies not be manipulated by them. Self-control our brain waves to better instant-erase pain and suffering, instant-stimulate pleasures and ecstasies visions and dreams and total recall of any experience in the past.

Let us also by implanting electrodes reinforce and expand tele-psychic communication. To plug in directly without words or gestures to other human consciousnesses. To plug in to fuse and defuse to merge and separate. To be one and to be many. To be alone and to be unalone. For me to be you and for you to be me. Here is a way to allay human loneliness and biological isolation.

Let us implant miniature computers in our bodies so we can store limitless information enabling us to retrieve it at will and instant-solve complex problems anytime anyplace.

Let us dispense with the hair on our heads attaching instead a solar cap which can draw on solar energy helping us remain energized (nourished) forever.

Let us insert a Dacron-like synthetic or a chemical insulation under the skin to protect it from burning freezing tearing corroding. If this is not feasible then let us dispense with our skin altogether and devise a new casing durable nonperishable and fluid enough to easily alter its color patterns shapes.

In countless other ways we can and we will redo the human organism. This very day in research centers around the planet bio-engineers bio-cyberneticists pioneering medical doctors space scientists and others are at work devising new body organs new techniques of transplants and implants and other ways of improving the quality of human life and its adaptability to radically new environments.

—Immortality. **The greatest tragedy in the human condition is death. Death and its imminence has brought more sorrow suffering anxiety than all other forces combined.**

Each person dies many times. We not only bear the imminence of our own death but die a little with the death of everyone we love.

The most urgent human problem facing us is death. We must start from here. All other social problems are secondary. When we speak of priorities what is more urgent than this all-encompassing problem of death?

Death is now a greater tragedy than ever. So far as we know today death is an end. There is no afterlife— no heaven no paradise no hell no rebirth. Death is final. Once you die you will never be heard from again.

More than ever therefore it is urgent to overcome death.

The conquest of death is the single transcendent triumph which in one sweep will defuse all other human problems. When we attain physical immortality we will automatically have defused such age-old problems as violence crime wars disease poverty hunger competition alienation anxiety . . .

Once we attain immortality everything will be possible. The Upheaval we are launching against death is therefore the most urgent.

Until the early 1960s immortality was still a metaphysical concept. Then it began to move to the domain of science. Today in research centers around the planet millions of dollars are spent yearly in the upheaval against humanity's gravest crisis. The drive to redo the human body is ultimately aimed at overcoming death.

This upheaval against mortality now gaining momentum can be divided into two phases.

Phase One. Stop-gap measures to *forestall* death. These include—

Anti-aging Measures. Control of diet and systematic fasting. Rejuvenating hormones. Molecular manipulation. Preservative chemicals in the diet. Anti-aging pill. Rejuvenating ionized air. Low gravity simulation to decrease pressures on the heart and other organs. Replacement of dying vital organs through transplants. Regeneration of body parts. Flushing out the accumulation of waste in the cells. Immunosuppressant drugs to reverse blockage of cell reproduction.

Suspended Animation. Freezing the body immediately after death to be revived in the future.

Long-term Hibernation. A technique to retard aging while awaiting a time in the future when immortality itself can be attained.

Cloning. Depositing body cells in a Cell Bank or with a doctor. In case of accidental death the cells could be cloned to reproduce the exact genetic duplicate of the deceased insuring a kind of biological quasi-immortality.

Life-suit. A synthetic skin-tight one-piece unisex year-round garment. Built-in heating and air-conditioning to insure comfortable body temperature at all times. Fire-resistant and tear-proof. Instant inflatability to protect the wearer from drowning or in case of a crash or collision protect from injuries and death. A light transparent headgear with two-way transistor communication. The life-suit also includes a body-monitoring system connected to tele-medical centers for constant surveillance of body functions. In case of an imminent organ malfunction or any disorder the wearer is automatically advised to take the necessary precautions. In case of sudden death the temperature in the life-suit is instantly dropped to the coldest level to protect the body and particularly the brain from degenerating while awaiting cryonic suspension.

The above techniques do not by themselves insure immortality. They are simply stop-gap measures to help us gain time. For instance much progress has already been made in anti-aging methods. Scientists are now optimistic that by 1985 we will be able to postpone aging in a dramatic way. A great number of people will live to 150 years or more. But what if a person drowns is burned to death or killed in a crash? No anti-aging technique will help. Progress is also being made in cryonic suspension of life. But what if a person dies in an isolated area and the body cannot be frozen immediately. The damage to the brain will be irreversible and no freezing will help. What if the life-suit malfunctions? Phase One therefore while reassuring is hardly the answer.

Phase Two. The actual attainment of immortality. This is a longer-range movement—

Genetic Engineering. It will be possible in the coming decades to make extensive genetic modifications in the human body excising many of our perishable organs grafting or inserting instead entirely new body parts which will be self-regenerating or nondegenerating.

Cyborg. As I explained earlier we are already

replacing many body organs for human-created parts. This trend will persist till we have remade the entire human body. We will create esthetically attractive versatile durable bodies for the brain. (Still later we will learn to isolate the brain entirely miniaturize it when desired into an ever smaller and smaller unit till it becomes a minute particle—a trans-material life able to rematerialize in many forms and dematerialize again back and forth at will to belong to All-Time All-Space.)

It is this second phase in our upheaval against death we must strive for. Immortality is now a question of how and when—not if.

The present drive toward immortality is beginning to raise questions in people's minds. Where will we put everybody? That is hardly a problem. Once we attain immortality we will no longer need to procreate. We will strive to regenerate and perfect the living. Moreover as I already noted in the coming years we will continue to spread out inhabiting deserts and oceans, space stations and other planets. Space is limitless.

What about boredom and stagnation? These problems are predicated on our age-old conditioning and limited existences. Immortality and Space will lead to entirely new premises and potentials which may bring new kinds of problems but not a perpetuation of the old.

What if I don't want to live forever? That is your privilege. Immortality must not be an imposition. Nor must death. We want to strive for our individual right to live as long as *we* want. Ten years one hundred years a million a billion—forever. Or to suspend life for an interval then go on living. We want to win the right to self-determination about life itself. We cannot make decisions about life so long as we do not make decisions about death.

It is precisely this ancient orientation to death which hinders us from launching a global crash movement to overcome mortality. Humans are still too death-oriented too guilt-ridden too submissive and fatalistic to demand immortality. To even hope for it.

The Future will look back on our times amazed that humanity was so close to attaining immortality yet having done so little.

Political leaders and self-styled revolutionaries still exhort their followers to fight to the end. "If you have nothing to die for you have nothing to live for" they say. These leaders and the movements they launch are bogged down in the death-oriented Old World.

They still cannot see that life itself is the greatest Revolution. That to lose your life is to lose all rights all freedoms—everything.

Then too some social scientists and philosophers still urge that we *accept* death. "Alone among the living man knows that he will die" say the existential psychologists.

Alone among the living we humans now know or ought to know that we can *overcome* death.

In all their exhortations to *accept* pain and death I hear echoes of Old World resignation. Perhaps even a desire for death. They have made a virtue out of what was a necessity.

We Up-Wingers are building a New World which is resigned to nothing—no pain suffering or death.

We want to overcome death. Do not ask us to accept death. We are prepared only to accept life.

The day will come when the death of one single human—any human—will be so rare and tragic that the news flashed across the planet will stun humanity.

Let us hasten that day when death will be something of our past—ahead of us only Life.

beyond utopia

Contemporary philosophers state that we humans are
striving to be god. Others more critical admonish us
for arrogantly "playing god." They warn of dire
consequences.

These critics are absurd. We humans do not want to
be god or to play god.

We aspire to much more.

God was a crude concept—vengeful wrathful
destructive. We humans want to evolve beyond god.

Is all this utopian? Unrealistic? This is what pessimists and other detractors of humanity are quick to charge.

But what is utopia? What is realism?

In 1950 the very concept of living with a new heart or kidney was considered unrealistic utopian. So too the idea of actually visiting another planet.

In our times realism means keeping pace with our rapidly changing situation aware that what is unrealistic or utopian today is reality next month or next year.

The modern world has already evolved beyond utopia. For centuries utopianism has been predicated on the puritan conditions of hard work and the simple collective life. As I have already explained we renounce the mystique of hard work and the simple life. We aspire to Leisure and Creativity and the Fluid Universal Life. Above all we strive for new dimensions in human existence—we want to extend ourselves through infinity and eternity.

This cosmic dimension is just beginning to unfold. It could not have possibly been anticipated by *any* thinkers, utopian or other.

Utopianism is now too modest. We Up-Wingers are beyond utopia—beyond the most utopian dreams of the most utopian philosophers.

We are Cosmic.

Are we moving too fast? Some social critics think so. They contend that people are having difficulties coping with rapid change.

What amazes me is not that a few people have difficulty coping with some aspects of change but the ease with which most people adapt to change—even to monumental breakthroughs.

In just the last two decades the entire world has undergone phenomenal upheavals. In rapid succession we have sailed through several *ages.* We have coped remarkably well. Once change has taken place most people adapt. They then resist new advances.

The overriding phenomenon today is not the problem of *coping* with rapid progress. But the clamor for more and more progress. This is clearly evident in all the spreading youth movements women's movements the drive to regionalism the biological upheaval the technological breakthroughs the rapid emergence of universal values and institutions . . .

We humans are remarkably adaptable and resilient.

This adaptability itself is daily spreading as people grow up *conditioned* to rapid change. The more we advance the more we want to advance.

It is neither possible nor even desirable to slow down progress. We should strive instead to *guide* our forward thrust.

This is not a time to hold back to slow down to waver or to flounder in despair. We want to move on. We want to get on with it.

We have too many old problems to resolve. Too many new visions to fulfill.

This is a glorious time in human evolution. An age of exploding potentials. We are only now beginning to test our wings.

In this late twentieth century we Up-Wingers are launching an upheaval greater than any movement greater than any revolution in our entire past. This is a Cosmic Upheaval which will not simply catapult us to a higher history as the visionary Nietzsche had

anticipated, but to something far more transcendent—
a higher evolution.

Let us not be afraid of vision and hope. It was the
daring of visionaries that has brought us this far—from
gloomy primordial marshes to where we are today—
reaching for the galaxies reaching for immortality.